LIFE BY
FAL

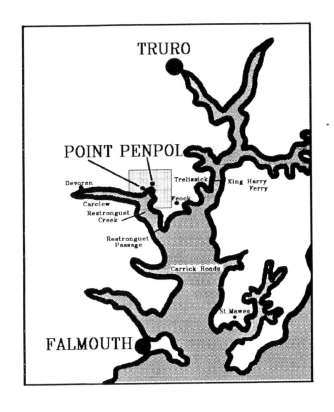

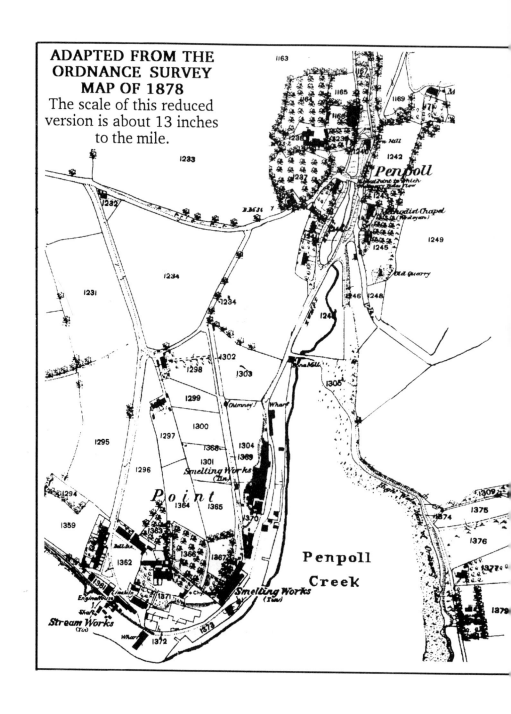

ADAPTED FROM THE
ORDNANCE SURVEY
MAP OF 1878
The scale of this reduced
version is about 13 inches
to the mile.

LIFE BY THE FAL

YEARS OF CHANGE AT

POINT AND PENPOL

BY

VIV ACTON

First published 1993
by
LANDFALL PUBLICATIONS
Landfall, Penpol, Devoran, Truro, Cornwall TR3 6NW
Telephone: Truro (0872) 862581

Copyright © V.M. Acton 1993

British Library Cataloguing-in-Publication Data.
A catalogue record for this book is available from the British Library.

ISBN 1 873443 10 2

ACKNOWLEDGEMENTS

This book could only have been attempted with the help willingly given to me by so many people. For their memories, mementoes and family knowledge I am indebted to Mr. Ralph Bird, Mr. Alan Burley, Mr. and Mrs. Reg Crocker, Mr. and Mrs. Graham Crocker, Mr. and Mrs. Ivor Dunstan, Messrs. Brian and Paul Ferris, Mrs. Nancy Hibbert, Mrs. Hazel Michell, Mr. and Mrs. Russell Michell, Mr. and Mrs. David Rees and Mr. and Mrs. Frank Trebilcock; for information on their houses to Mr. Giles Carne, Mr. and Mrs. Nicholas Humby and Mrs. Sheila de Burlet, and Mr. and Mrs. Pat Hunt; to Mr. Kenneth Brown for his detailed interpretation of the painting of the tin mine at Point; to Mr. Justin Brooke for his information on the industrial past; to Captain George Hogg for his advice and knowledge about the ships built locally; to Mr. A. Hitchens Unwin for his information on the corn mill; to Mr. and Mrs. Arthur Irwin for showing me files from the Carnon Downs Old Cornwall Society; to Mr. and Mrs. Christopher Kingston for the record books of Penpoll Methodist Church, an invaluable source; to the ever-helpful staff of the Cornwall Record Office, the Royal Institution of Cornwall, Truro City Reference Library and the Cornish Studies Library. I would also like to thank all those past writers in the local newspapers who have given me so many insights into life of a hundred years or so ago. There are also others too numerous to mention, who wittingly or unwittingly gave me clues for my researches.

If my husband, Bob, had not initiated me into the joys (and frustrations) of a word processor I would never have had the patience to write this down. His drawings enliven the text, he has uncomplainingly proof-read and corrected, amongst other things, my errant punctuation, he has bravely undertaken to publish the book, a vital necessity, and if this were not enough he has also done kitchen duty.

I have done my best to avoid errors but if there are any I apologise and take full responsibility.

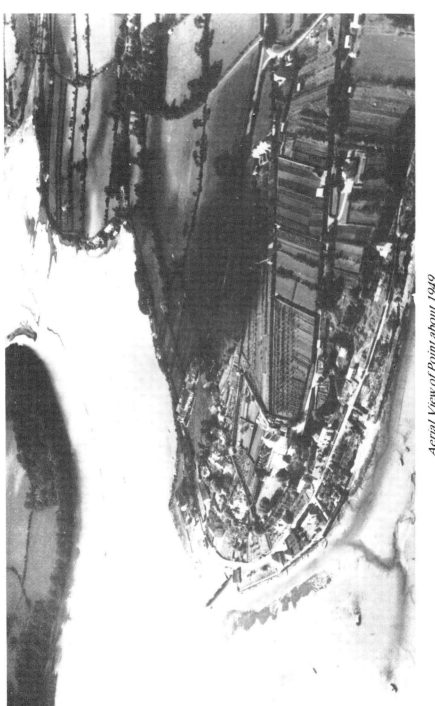

Aerial View of Point about 1949
Note Point (Daniell's) Quay where Penpol Creek joins Restronguet Creek, and the market gardens
on the land above the village.   *(Courtesy Mrs. V. Beckton)*

Looking across Penpol Creek to Point
Notice the lead smelter stack still standing and the newer one on the right
for the working tin smelter.

(Courtesy Mr. and Mrs. R. Michell)

Point beach and Chypit

CONTENTS

PART 1: MAINLY WORK

PART 2: PARTLY LEISURE

INTRODUCTION

One hundred and fifty years ago the view from my window, if it had existed then, looking out over Penpol Creek would have been of the rough roofs of the lead smelter buildings, of sparks flaring up from the furnaces, and smoke belching out from the cluster of chimneys obscuring the creek busy with sailing barges, schooners and small shore craft scurrying to and fro. The heavy thump of stamps machines crushing up the ore from Carnon Mine would have echoed across the water, mixed with hammering from the nearby boatyard, clanging from the smelter and shouts from the quay below as more ore was barrelled on to the waiting boats.

As I look out now a sailboard skims across to Carnon Yard, masts of leisure boats rock gently in the breeze, a couple stroll slowly along the Old Tram Road and our black and white blackbird perches momentarily on the ridge of the house below before flying off into the fir trees edging the garden. Change is the theme of this account of Penpol and Point and this is the most dramatic. Houses with their neat gardens now stand where fifty years ago small fields hedged with pittosporum, were colourful with daffodils, violets or anemones. Changes are deplored by some and appreciated by others; the following account will attempt to trace some of these and the people connected with them.

It would not be true to say that no-one from Point would marry anyone from Penpol, as is said about Camborne and Redruth, but their separate identities and those of Chycoose and Trolver should be emphasised, even if today this separateness is not so obvious.

The spelling of names can be an emotive subject. In this area there were families of Stephens and Stevens, Michell and Mitchell, but the records are not consistent in showing these differences. The changes in the spelling of Penpol - or is it Penpoll? - are perhaps even more problematic. I have kept to the former version as it is in more general use today and is probably the more correct form of the Cornish language. However, where Penpoll is used as part of a longer name or in a quotation, I have used this version.

Mr. Searle and Mr. Colliver are in their boats off Point (Daniell's) Quay. Elijah Searle later demolished the tall lead smelter stack. Notice the working tin smelter on the right. (Courtesy Mr. and Mrs. R. Michell)

PART 1

MAINLY WORK

Point Green Today
Cottages built for the quay and smelter workers.
Bath's shop was at the left hand end of the cottages on the right.
The pump was not erected until between the wars.

Point and Penpol in the 1920s
Above: in 1842 Lord Falmouth owned this land in Point.
Below: in 1842 the foreground was Daniell property with Lemon land
on the far side of the Penpol Valley. (Courtesy Mr. and Mrs. R. Michell)

THE LAND

Hunted over, pastured on, cropped from, quarried into and mined under; the land has been exploited and changed to such an extent over the years that most of our countryside is as much man-made as the towns. The land around Penpol and Restronguet Creeks is no exception.

LANDOWNERS
".. liberty for the said John Vivian his heirs, servants, friends and followers to hunt, hawk, fish or fowl in and upon the said premises."

This reference to a landowner's right to hawk and hunt has a medieval ring about it, but it is much more modern, coming from a lease of the nineteenth century for Lynwood, the property along the Old Tram Road just below Chycoose. It is some indication that change could be slow where the rights of landowners were concerned.

Land was owned by a small minority of men, who for hundreds of years used it as a basis for their income and power. Soon after 1066 William the Conqueror granted about two-thirds of all the land in Cornwall, including some of the land around Penpol and Restronguet Creeks, to his half-brother Robert of Mortain, and most of the rest went to the church. In due course Cornwall become an earldom, the title usually being given to a member of the royal family, and then in 1337 Edward I created the Duchy of Cornwall with his son, Edward the Black Prince, as the first holder of the title. The Duke of Cornwall, Prince Charles, still owns a lot of land and certain rights in the county.

Lands within the duchy were granted, not only to the church but also to a small number of families whose members often held administrative positions. No great medieval manor was centred on Penpol Creek, so there is no ruined castle or ancient manor house to excite our curiosity. In fact, just as the Penpol stream has, since 1873, divided the parish of Feock from the newer parish of Devoran, so it formed a dividing line between the huge estates of the medieval bishops of Exeter, based at Tregear in the Roseland, and the Domesday manor of Goodern. (Goodern Manor Farm is west of Playing Place.) Lands around Restronguet Creek were held by the Cardinham family of Cardinham near Bodmin and later by the Bodrugan family from near Dodman Point, until the upheavals of the Wars of the Roses in the late fifteenth century.

These landowners, and those who came later, would also expect other rights from the land they leased apart from hunting and fishing. The same Chycoose lease mentions timber, bark and charcoal. Timber was in short supply but under increasing demand from at least Tudor times, not only for fuel, house and boat building, but also for the mining industry as it developed, and

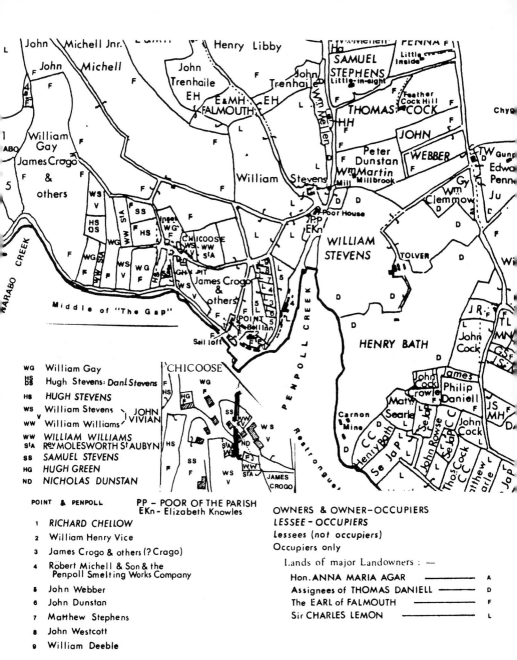

Part of the Tithe Map for 1842 showing the landowners, leaseholders and occupiers. This carefully executed map was first produced and published by the Feock Local History Group.

charcoal was used for smelting the tin in blowing houses. Bark was used for leather tanning. (Croggons' Tannery in Grampound is the only one in the country still using traditional oak bark methods.) The stripping of bark from the trees around the Fal Estuary for this purpose only died out fairly recently. Mr. Gunn of Coombe, a mile or so away, used stilts to cross the river mud to reach the trees on the far side at low tide. The oak trees still clinging on to the steep sides of the Penpol Valley were probably planted because of this demand.

As tin and then copper mining developed, land provided another potential source of income for landowners, and leases of the late eighteenth and the nineteenth centuries included not only the mineral rights but increasingly the rights for processing minerals; but more of this in a later section.

By the nineteenth century wealth generated from the mines gave a chance for new men to become landowners, for to own land brought social status and political power both locally and nationally. The Tithe Map of 1842 shows that the ownership of land at Chycoose was entirely with the older families of Boscawen (Lord Falmouth), Vivian and St. Aubyn, but around Penpol Creek the three owners were Lord Falmouth and two of the "new men." Sir Charles Lemon of Carclew on the far side of Restroguet Creek had inherited the fortune his great-grandfather William Lemon had made from mining and smelting, and owned land to the north and west of Penpol Creek. Thomas Daniell had inherited the Trelissick estate, which included land on the east of the creek, from his father Ralph Allen Daniell, whose own father had been William Lemon's chief clerk and had founded the family fortune. By the mid-nineteenth century that fortune had waned; Thomas was living abroad, a declared bankrupt, having mortgaged all the estate to Lord Falmouth.

The land was the main source of revenue for many landowners, so the rents were important. Leases of 99 years, or for three lives, had been common, but they were not very flexible for the owners. At Penpol in the late eighteenth century, as in many of the larger farms, it became more usual to have leases for 14 or 21 years, when rents could be changed according to the circumstances.

Farming went through good and bad times, as it still does today. The wars with France in the late eighteenth and early nineteenth centuries created corn shortages in Britain, made worse by the rapidly expanding population. Food riots broke out, the most serious being in 1812, when the price of bread was higher than many could afford. This was the staple food, the basis of most meals for the poor; but while people like the miners suffered, farmers were doing well, putting more and more land to the plough for growing corn.

Landowners took advantage of this by raising rents as is shown in the leases for Penpol Farm. In 1785, eight years before war broke out, the yearly rent was £34. In 1807 it more tnan doubled to £73. The end of the war in 1815 brought prices plummeting down and bad harvests made the situation worse for farmers. A lower rent of £52 and a short tenancy of only three years at Penpol perhaps reflects this. Landowners in parliament, suffering from reduced rents, passed the Corn Laws to keep up the price of corn by

IN FEOCK.

The FEE SIMPLE IN POSSESSION of all that TENEMENT called

C H Y C O O S E ,

In the occupation of Mr. W. H. Chellew, and his undertenants.

No. on Map.	Name of Field.		Quantity.	
		a.	r.	p.
700	The Breach	2	1	19
713	Higher Lambrose	1	1	20
714	Lower do.	1	0	22
726	Meadow	1	1	12
737	Gate Close	1	2	36
742	Garden	0	0	8
743	Working Close	2	0	8
725	Three Cottages	0	0	21
738	Plot now into 737	0	0	12
724	Cottage, Garden, Waste, &c.	0	0	8
727	Garden	0	0	32
696	Chycoose Croft	6	2	0
		16	3	38

This Tenement is situate near *Point*, and about half-a-mile only from *Devoran*; it abuts on Restronguit Creek, and the Railroad passes through a portion of the Land. One Acre of Chycoose Downs, unenclosed, belongs to the Tenement. There is a TIMBER POND also occupied with the above.

The FREEHOLD IN REVERSION of that newly erected

D W E L L I N G   H O U S E

and GARDEN, situate at CHYCOOSE aforesaid, held under Lease dated 28th September, 18-14, for 99 years, and now determinable on the deaths of Samuel Stephens, aged 42, John Stephens, 37, and Lavinia Stephens, 17, under the annual Conventionary Rent of £1.; and a Heriot of 5s. on the death of each Life.

No. 736   Dwelling House and Garden .... 0a.   1r.   16p.

Part of an 1858 Sale Catalogue for Chycoose
Note the reference to unenclosed land on Chycoose Downs, the Timber
Pond and the lease on three Stephens' lives for the house now known as
Lynwood. (C.R.O. WH 6460)

restricting imports. A recovery in trade and industry brought greater prosperity for many, again reflected in Penpol by only one change of family tenancy from 1820 to 1894.

Some landowners led the way in improving the standard of farming, which the demands of a rapidly growing population made vital. John Davies Gilbert, who bought the Trelissick estate in 1844, took an active interest in farming, both arable and pastoral. He exhibited Cornish wheat and barley seeds at the Great Exhibition in the Crystal Palace in 1851 and he improved the breed of sheep by introducing stock from his other estates in Sussex and building up a sizable herd. John Michell, who was farming at Tregoose at this time, also had corn seed on display in the Crystal Palace.

This trend had begun over a hundred years earlier, through the influence of such men as the Norfolk landowner Lord "Turnip" Townshend. (His nickname came from his encouraging the use of turnips as a field crop in rotation with corn and clover rather than any rude comment on his abilities or lack of them.) But the changes had been slow coming to Cornwall where farming was not such a vital part of the economy. In due course changes happened and it was the landowners who had the influence in parliament to pass the necessary acts. The following extract from the *West Briton* of August 30th 1811 gives an example of this.

"Notice is hearby given, that application will be made in the next session of parliament for leave to bring in a bill for inclosing, dividing and allotting, and also for extinguishing all tin work bounds, within or upon certain commons or waste lands commonly called Cosigarne Downs, Chicoose Commons, Cold-Wind Cross, Trevarth Common, Killiwherries Common, Feock Downs and Pennance Commons, situate in the several parishes of Gwennap, Kea and Feock in the county of Cornwall."

The hill ridges above Point and Penpol were open downland at this time, useful as a possible source of tin, for grazing sheep, gathering furze and for turbary, the right to cut turf for fuel, but no good for the more intensive farming that was now being demanded; land needed to be divided up and hedged. In 1818 Lord Falmouth's agent advertised Feock Downs for lease in lots of five to ten acres and soon it was all enclosed. Chycoose Common took longer and some was still open land in 1858 as a sale notice indicates. All this activity affected the tenant farmers, who were increasingly encouraged to improve their methods by the terms of the leases they were granted.

FARMS AND FARMING
"and also shall and will dress, manage and manure .....
according to custom or rules of Good Husbandry."

Farming settlements must have developed around the creeks during medieval times or perhaps earlier and some medieval documents have familiar names, as it was a common practice to call people after their home area. William de Penpol is recorded in 1275, and John de Penpol and John Tregoose in the Lay Subsidy Rolls of 1327. Chycoose is mentioned in the Patent Rolls of 1378. These rolls were official taxation and legal records.

These were only very small settlements. An early-seventeenth-century document records one tenement at Penpol (head of the creek) two at Tregoose (farmstead in the woods) and five at Chycoose (house in the woods), certainly not big enough to feature on Baptista Boazio's map of 1597. His "true Description of ye Great Baie of Falmouth" names Penpoel Cove, Tregouse Point and Tregouse Cove but shows no houses. Richard Carew's fascinating "Survey of Cornwall," produced a few years later, mentions no place between Truro and Falmouth Haven on the west of the Fal. Gascoigne's map of 1699 names Penpol and Trolver only.

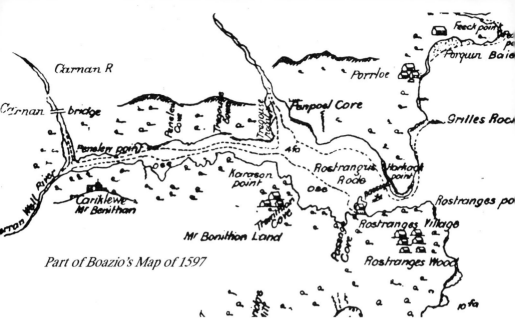

Part of Boazio's Map of 1597

The people living in these tenements were tenant farmers and some leases drawn up in the seventeenth and early eighteenth centuries are still in existence. The oldest one is dated 1638 for a property at Chycoose belonging to William Coryton in the manor of Landegay. This was a life leasehold for 99 years or for the lives of 3 named people. Although this form of lease died out for farms, it still remained in use well into the nineteenth century for houses, as other leases in Chycoose show, including the one for Lynwood, quoted at the very beginning.

Chycoose was a settlement of smallholders in the mid-nineteenth century, with most of the twelve or so householders depending on other occupations, such as Samuel Stephens, waterman, Hugh Stephens, carpenter, and Hugh Green, leadsmelter. William Gay was the only one described as a farmer and he had only 14 acres. Later on William Daniell had a much more sizable farm of 30 acres, which grew to 70 acres by 1881. Later still two farms operated here for a time, "Chypit" and "Chycoose Croft," but by 1910 Henry Collins was farming both.

In Penpol and Point the Tithe Map of 1842 shows that several people had some land for cultivating or for keeping a few animals. The land on the western side of Ropewalk (Black Road) was divided into seven small fields, used by people like James Crago, beershop keeper, John Webber, wheelwright, and John Dunstan, porter. Some years later the innkeeper, Thomas Kempe, and the timber merchant, William Chellew, were also described as farmers, so many people were still close to the land.

The three main farms around Penpol Creek were Tregoose, Penpol and Trolver, with Tresithick and later Feather Cock Hill on either side of the higher slopes of the Penpol Valley. Tregoose was a sizable farm of about 100 acres in the nineteenth century. The present attractive house is thought to

16

date from the eighteenth century. but there must have been a medieval predecessor somewhere in the area. Penpol was farmed with part of Trolver in the earlier nineteenth century and was also about 100 acres, but then it reduced to about half the size as Trolver more than doubled its acreage to support two farm households.

Farming practices in Cornwall were often wasteful until two hundred or so years ago, but perhaps acceptable for a static or slow-growing population. It had been usual to clear land of vegetation by burning, manure it with sea sand, plough it, crop it for a year or so and then leave it to revert to grass and furze. But during the eighteenth century the population began to grow rapidly at a time when Cornwall was helping to lead the way in the far-reaching changes of the Industrial Revolution. Changes were needed in farming to meet the new demands, and these were also far-reaching enough to be called a revolution. Leases that were drawn up for farmers in Chycoose and Penpol illustrate some of these changes very well.

A lease for Penpol Farm in 1781 mentions that the lessee was not to take more than three crops of corn successively without new dressing and that straw was to be used for foddering cattle or for converting to dung "for the better manuring and improving of the same". Four years later similar instructions for good husbandry were included as the quotation at the beginning shows. But thirty two years later the lease is more specific in the requirements. The leaseholder was expected to use "for every acre of tilled land eight cartloads of Good Sea Sand or fifty Bushells of well burnt lime". This was in addition to "other dung and manure". It was stressed that no more than two crops were to be taken after such a dressing.

This emphasis on soil improvement was typical of the Agrarian Revolution and these leases show the changes in ideas. Sea sand had been used in Cornwall long before this time to counteract the acid in the soil and its use obviously continued. In an agreement of 1824 Samuel Stephens of Chycoose, who had fields beside the creek, allowed Charles Fox of Perranwharf use of his land, but kept for himself a plot to bring ashore "manure sand". However the 1817 Penpol lease mentions lime as an alternative.

The Lime Kiln

Lime had been burned in Cornwall for a long time as Carew's "Survey of Cornwall", published in 1602, shows. "They make lime ..... either by burning a great quantity thereof together, with a fervent fire of furse, or by maintaining a continual though lesser heat with stone coal in smaller kilns." He does not say that this was used on the land. It had other uses, such as for cement in building, and its use on soil came later. It presumably would not be mentioned in the 1817 lease if it had not been easily available then and Point has a very good example of a small kiln.

Until quite recently the kiln was unrecognisable behind a thick covering of ivy but much of that has now been cut back to reveal its origins. Like so many of the kilns still to be seen around the coasts of Cornwall it is situated near the water close to the quay. Limestone was brought by ship, usually from near

Lime Kiln by Point Quay
Notice the iron shaft of the Restronguet Tin Stream Works showing through the mud of Restronguet Creek.

Plymouth, and the coal, or culm, for burning it came across the water from South Wales. The sturdy, stone structure is built into the hillside so that there was easy access to load from the top. The inverted cone inside was filled with layers of limestone and culm and the whole process was started by a fire in the arched opening below. The lime burner then raked out the burnt lime and slaked it, while more was loaded into the top.

Lime burning was often done by itinerant men, but Point had its own resident burner, John Hockin, living at Rope House in the mid-nineteenth century. This could be a very dangerous process both for the lime burner and for anyone else trying to take advantage of the heat, as these two extracts from the *West Briton* of 1819 and 1841 show.

"On Friday evening last, two men who were left to attend to a lime kiln belonging to J.P.Peters, Esq. at Philleigh, were overpowered, as it is supposed, by the gas which arose from the kiln, as they were pressing down the burning lime with an iron bar, in order to put more on top. They fell on the burning mass, and the bodies were found next morning reduced to ashes; nothing remaining but part of the scull of each. Both were married and have left children."

"On Sunday, the 4th instant, a little girl, about five years old, daughter of Mr. Paine, of the Coast Guard, at Portloe, was unfortunately burnt to death, by attempting to take a roasted potatoe * from a lime-kiln."
*(Ex-Vice-President Dan Quayle could take comfort from this spelling!)

18

It would seem that the lime kiln at Point was connected with the farmer, John Michell at Tregoose, because the Feock Church Book records him as paying rates of 3s 4d for it in 1832, but the lime was presumably available for other local farmers to buy.

The lime trade gradually declined after 1850 as the Plymouth chemical industry began producing artificial and chemical "manure". The Point kiln had probably stopped being used by the time the tin mine was established beside it in the early 1870s. In the 1871 census John Hockin was described as a "labourer" and had moved to Chycoose and no other lime burner is recorded, although the Ordnance Survey map does not describe it as "old" until the 1906 edition.

There are two other indications of the efforts made to improve soil at this time. One of the small fields at Point was called Marl Pit Field. This could refer to the practice of marling fields with a mixture of clay and lime. As this field was not far from the lime kiln it might have been connected with it in this way. The second indication was the building of a tide mill in the upper part of Penpol Creek.

The Tide Mill

A 99-year lease was granted in 1829 to William Stevens, farmer at Penpol, for "a plot of ground on the beach immediately under the hedge between Penpoll Croft and a field called Park-an-Walken". This field is where the newer houses in Penpol have now been built, overlooking the higher part of the creek. Bones were crushed here, an effective fertiliser, using the power of the tides to drive the machinery. A dam was built across the creek where it narrows, to form what is still known as "Bone Mill Pool," useful now as a winter haven for boats. Water from here was released from time to time to scour out the navigation channel beside the quays.

A few remains of this mill structure can be seen in the narrow gap between the dam and the western shore, and no doubt the granite blocks now used as stepping stones were once part of it. The mill is mentioned in the leases for the smelting house as late as 1880 but for how long it was used is unclear. The Ordnance Survey map of about 1878 shows it, but only the stepping stones are recorded in the 1906 edition.

The Corn Mill

For many years Penpol had its own water mill for grinding corn. When this was first built is not known but a document of 1630 records the customary tithes for Feock Church, "for one Mill called Penpol Mill to paye yearely Two shillinges at Easter". It was connected with the manor of Trevilla, owned by Robert Trefusis in the mid-eighteenth century when there were two grist mills* here. (See the extract below.) This later became Daniell property. Little can be seen now, but in the lush undergrowth just above the bridge are the remains of the leat which carried water to it from higher up the stream, and the nearby name of Millbrook gives a reminder of the past. The last recorded miller was the appropriately named William Mellen, who died in 1864; the Cornish word for "mill" is "melyn."

* Mr A. H. Unwin tells me this probably means two pairs of stones in one mill building.

19

The Corn Mill at Penpol
1568 "Rentall of the Manor of Trevylla ..... Penpole Myll. The heir of Trefusis esquyer in Knightes Service 2/6."
(Courtesy Penpoll Methodist Church)

Penpol Farm 1928.   The roundhouse was still there then, but few apple trees.
(Courtesy Mr. and Mrs. R. Michell)

Marion Chegwyn, who lived in Penpol until her death about 20 years ago, wrote: "The corn mill was situated on the higher side of the bridge with a small cottage joining it. I've heard my mother talk of going over for seconds," coarse flour no doubt. All I can remember are the large wheels and grinding stones and parts of the walls of the cottage and garden, now entirely obliterated."

Cider

The photograph of Penpol Farm shows a small, round building attached to a barn. Round houses like this were often built in the earlier nineteenth century to house horse-powered mechanisms for threshing corn, cutting chaff or crushing apples. Penpol had apple orchards, as the sale notice in the *Sherborne Mercury* of May 14th 1753 shows, which could produce "30 hogsheads of cyder." (A hogshead was about 54 gallons.) The Tithe Map of 1842 shows three orchards around the house, so perhaps the apples were crushed here for making cider, a popular country drink.

ON Tuefday the 29th Day of May Inftant, by three o' Clock in the Afternoon, at the Houfe of Mr William Courtis, being the Sign of the King's Head in the Borough of Truro, in the County of Cornwall, a Survey will be held for the Sale and Difpofal of the Remainder of two feveral Terms of 99 Years, the one determinable on three Lives, of and in a certain Tenement called Penpol, in the Parish of Feock, in the fame County; Confifting of a neat new built fafhed Dwelling Houfe, with a walled Courtlage, in the Occupation of Mrs. Johanna Tonken; a Farm Houfe and convenient Outhoufes, about fifty Acres of Ground, and as much Orchards to have produced thirty Hogsheads of Cyder in one Seafon, now in the Occupation of Roger Collins. The other determinable on one Life, of and in the tenement of Penpol Mills, contiguous to the former, and confifting of a new Dwelling Houfe, Mill Houfe, Stable and rwo Grist Mills, two Moors, and all the Orchards under the Mill River, now in the Occupation of Richard Allen; all fituate on a Creek, a Branch of the River Fal, just by Reftrongett, alias Stranguidge Passage, very convenient for landing Sea Sand and other Dressing, within five Miles of Truro and Falmouth, and three of Penryn, from either of which Place, the Paffage by Water, as well as the Road by Land is very pleafant and commodious, all late belonging to Captain Richard Blewett, deceased. -- Any Person defirous of further Particulars may apply to Mr. Abraham Hall, Attorney in Falmouth, or to the faid Roger Collins on the Premifes.
N.B. The Houfe, Courtlage, and Garden in the Occupation of Mrs. Tonken, may be purchafed with or without the other Parts of the Premifes.   *(Sherborne Mercury* May 14th 1753)

MASTER AND MAN

During the nineteenth century Agricultural Societies were formed, as at Probus, holding annual shows which were well reported in the local press. The larger Bath and West Show was held at Truro in 1861. These organisations would help spread the new ideas, such as the increasing use of mechanisation. Cornwall's great engineer, Richard Trevithick, had helped to lead the way by designing and building a steam-powered threshing machine for Sir Christopher Hawkins of Trewithen near Probus in 1812. Improvements like this would slowly reduce the need for labour. How much labour a farmer would have to employ would also depend on the size of his family, as sons and daughters often contributed towards the family enterprise.

In 1841 John Michell at Tregoose had a teenage son and daughter and two living-in farm workers, Sally Jose and her teenage son William. There were other Joses living nearby at Chycoose, who seem to have been more of Sally's children, with the eldest, a girl, also described as an agricultural labourer. These seem to be the only examples of women as farm workers in the area, although more might well have helped in the busy times like harvest.

21

At Trolver in 1861 there were two farming households. Edward Bath had sixty acres, but only employed one man. He must have been very hard working because the eldest of his four children was only thirteen. Next door to him was Thomas Mitchell (Michell) with forty-eight acres, employing one man and two boys and in addition having four teenage sons. After Edward Bath's tragic death (see below), the Michells seem to have farmed all of Trolver, with the two eldest sons later taking over from their father.

William Williams, farmer at Penpol, was eighty-seven years old in 1891. His household consisted of one daughter in her fifties and one female servant. This was very different from thirty years earlier when he had first taken over the tenancy. Then he had a wife, four daughters, one son and a living-in farm worker; but his son never had the chance to renew the tenancy because he was drowned at the age of twenty-one. There were three farm labourers living nearby, whom he probably employed; one of these was John Hall.

He came from a family of farm workers. His grandfather and father had lived at Tregew a mile or so away. His father had died at the young age of twenty-four of a brain disease, believed by the family to be the results of lead poisoning, when John was little more than one year old. Times must have been hard for the young widow with two small children to bring up. Grandfather Hall was unlikely to be able to offer much help on a farm worker's wage and her own father, a coastguard officer, was possibly in little better circumstances. John married when he was about twenty four and it was some time after this that he moved to Penpol from Harcourt. He and his wife had a large family including a son, Charles, who himself died at a young age from poisoning, this time because of the effects of mustard gas suffered during the First World War.

THE BATH TRAGEDY
"FATAL TRAP ACCIDENT NEAR TRURO

About seven o'clock on Saturday evening last, Mr. Edward Bath of Trolver Farm, Feock, and his wife left Truro in a pony cart for their home, their route being by way of the new Falmouth turnpike-road. After stopping at Plynt's Barn turnpike to pay the toll they proceeded onward, but on the steep descent the pony became restless, jumping and kicking. Mr. Bath tried in vain to pull him in, and an effort by Mr. Hugh Pearce, who was walking on the road, also proved unsuccessful. The driver then pulled the pony towards the hedge ...... but in making this attempt the trap was capsized, and both Mr. and Mrs. Bath were thrown out violently." (*West Briton,* April 1872)

Caroline Bath had terrible head injuries and died soon afterwards in the Infirmary where they were both taken, and Edward died a few days later at home.

His father, Henry Bath, had been farming at Trolver by 1832 and by 1851, when he was 62 years old, he had given up most of the farm to his son, Edward, retiring for some years to one of the cottages he had built on his land overlooking the creek. This area was known for some time as Bathtown and these older cottages, now enlarged and modernised, can still be detected

John Hall, his wife Louisa and their four eldest children, Nellie, Emma,
Elizabeth and Edith in 1892
They had eight more children including Charles born in 1894.
(Courtesy Mrs. N. Hibbert)

amongst the newer houses. He survived the tragic death of his son by three years.

An account of the accident given by their great-granddaughter gives more details. Edward's wife, Caroline, had dreamt the night before of a "*Ganges* man," a cadet from the training ship *Ganges* in Falmouth harbour, and of being in a dark place calling to her daughter Clarinda. The following day she and her husband had gone to town with one of his lively horses. "Edward had the ability to handle any horse however fresh and strong - indeed the friskier the better." On their return they offered a lift to a mariner friend, John Trethowan, but he refused it.

As they were going down Arch Hill behind the prancing horse, a *Ganges* man rushed out to grab the reins, thinking that it was out of control. (Presumably Mr. Hugh Pearce.) The horse reared in fright and fell over on top of them. Caroline died in hospital calling to her daughter. Edward, wanting to break the news to his daughter himself, walked the four miles or so home but died shortly afterwards. (The newspaper reports this differently saying that he was driven home by Mr. Hugo, a Feock man, who had come on the scene of the accident and had taken them to hospital.)

This must have been a terrible time for their daughter Clarinda, a young widow with two sons, who had been living with her parents. She later married John Trethowan, who might so easily have been killed with them.

Neither of Edward's sons continued with the farm after this. The elder, William, had emigrated to America and the younger, Edward (Ned), was only 17 years old. But their elder daughter, Mary, had married William Michell whose father was a next-door-neighbour, already farming part of Trolver land. He now took on some of the extra land with the help of his two elder sons, Thomas and Ralph, and William and Mary continued to live at Trolver for some time, so a Bath connection still continued there.

CONCLUSION

The last twenty or so years of the nineteenth century were very difficult ones in Cornwall not just in agriculture with competition from the vast prairies of America, but also because of the collapse in mining. Farming had not been the main source of labour but it had helped to underpin the economy. However amid the gloom there was one small glimmer of light and that was the growth of market gardening and flower growing. This was soon to become a very important part of the economy of Point and Penpol providing a new way to use the land and bringing much-needed employment. (See later section.)

Bone Mill Pool, Penpol, in the mid-1920s
Penpol Farm is on the extreme right.   (Courtesy Mr. and Mrs. R. Michell)

The Old Tram Road in the early 1950s
"Old Muggins" the pilchard seller with his pony and trap. The rails have gone
but the road has not yet been surfaced. (Courtesy Mr. and Mrs. R. Crocker)

CHAPTER TWO

TRANSPORT

If you were faced with roads thick with mud squelching up to the wheel hubs or disappearing altogether on the bare downs, with flooded fords and few signs, would you regard travel by boat as a safer, quicker and more comfortable alternative? This would be the choice facing people for hundreds of years, and for many water was better than land, especially if they needed to transport anything in bulk. The drowned river valleys of the south coast of Cornwall, with the tides penetrating far inland, were an aid rather than a barrier to transport in the past and the Fal river and estuary with its creeks spreading out north, east and west were once busy with boats of all types.

1) SHIPPING
"There were quays all the way along from Point to Penpol."
Coastal and cross-channel trade in this area must date back to early times. It would be interesting to speculate on Phoenician boats nosing their way into Restronguet Creek to find tin, but for the fact that no evidence has been found of them either here or anywhere else in Cornwall, in spite of the oft-repeated stories. However the tin trade certainly brought boats to Cornwall, and it was this and especially the copper boom of the late eighteenth and the nineteenth centuries that brought most shipping to Point and Penpol.

Point Quay
It was the building of Point Quay at Tregoose Point which signalled the start of much more intensive shipping activity in this area. Here the land juts out towards the deep water channel where Penpol Creek joins Restronguet Creek, making an ideal site. Point was a late developer compared with Penpol or Chycoose because its origins are connected with this quay built in the late eighteenth century.

Thomas Daniell, formerly William Lemon's clerk, had taken over many of the Lemon business interests after William's death in 1760, and had built up his own powerful industrial and mercantile empire. One part of this was the development of Daniell's Quay as it soon became known. The mines of Gwennap needed the shortest land routes to transport the copper ore to the water for shipment to the smelters of South Wales and to bring Welsh coal back to work the powerful mine engines. The south coast anchorages were safer than those on the exposed north coast, even if the voyage was longer around Land's End. Soon the waters around Point would have echoed with the busy activity of the quay.

How much of the original stonework of the quay is still in existence is difficult to say as it was enlarged over the years, but the vertical layering still to be seen is perhaps a sign of the early building. Dressed granite blocks edge the quay, but most of the stone is killas, possibly quarried from the lower slopes of the hill above Penpol Creek.

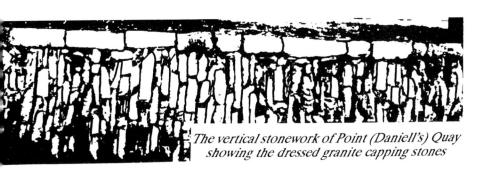

The vertical stonework of Point (Daniell's) Quay showing the dressed granite capping stones

This was the only quay here for some years although there were many similar ones in the other creeks such as Pill and Roundwood. However as the land on the western side of Penpol Creek belonged to Sir William Lemon, grandson of the founder of the Lemon fortunes, it was not too long before plans for this area were being made.

The 1807 lease for Penpol Farm allowed Sir William "to erect and make any Engine Stamping Mills and other Edifices.....for better working and discovery of mines or making ores merchantable." Nothing was done then but ten years later a new lease excluded "all that one field or croft commonly called by the name of Point Field or Penpol Croft. This to be granted to John Swan gentleman," and in that same year a 21 year lease was made with "John Swan gentleman" for this land to build "Quays Wharfs Jetties Storehouses and other conveniences." (Lawyers did not seem to know about the use of commas in leases!)

Threats and Rivalry

The building of the new quay was soon under way, and it must have been completed very quickly because it was ready for use on January 1st 1818. It had a long frontage on Penpol Creek and "may be approached by vessels of 160 tons burthen or upwards." *(West Briton,* Aug. 1828) But the Daniell business empire did not welcome competition at such close quarters; Lemon Quay, as it was called, was only a few yards away from the older quay and access to it involved crossing Daniell's Quay. Moves were made to try and stop this.

Lemon and Point Quays,

RESTRONGUET RIVER,

January 1, 1818.

JOHN SWAN and Co. are ready to receive COPPER ORES to be shipped for Wales, from Lemon Quay and to purchase any Coals brought by the Ships that may be sent to carry away the Ores; and the Mines and the Country supplied on reasonable Terms.

A fresh imported Cargo of

Norway Timber and Deals,

Now discharging:

And a large assortment of IRON, NAILS, and other Articles, wanted for the Mines.

New and twice-laid CORDAGE, of the best quality, and 20 cwt. to the ton.

————————————From the *West Briton*

Thomas Daniell had notices put up "threatening the carriers with Law proceedings for Trespass." This action did not deter the carriers or John Swan, who wrote a letter to Sir William's steward to report the successful opening. "I have pleasure to inform you that Lemon Quay was opened for the reception of Copper Ores...and William Williams of Devoran was the first man who had the honour about one o'clock in the morning ...to bring his pair of horses to the Quay - indeed it was a contention among the carriers who should first arrive and before three o'clock upwards of a hundred mules had deposited their burthens in the Crown Copper Company's Hutch."

How many people in Point slept that night? Men would have been working on the quay unloading the ore by lamplight; women, huddled in shawls against the winter night, probably clustered at their doorways watching the mules troop past, wondering if there was going to be any trouble, and no doubt children peeped from the windows to watch the excitement.

John Swan's letter referred to the attempts made to block this. "We have continued to bring the mules down Point Road and across Point Quay to Lemon Quay notwithstanding all opposition which Mr. Daniell has endeavoured to throw in our way." The Daniell notices were signed by one Thomas Rogers, " a person (for I cannot describe him as a gentleman)," as John Swan wrote. Thomas Rogers is to be accused of other questionable practices four years later. (See section on smuggling.)

The Shipping Boom

As Cornish mining boomed during the middle years of the nineteenth century, so shipping increased and the land along the western side of Penpol Creek was further developed until quays stretched for most of its length. It might be difficult for us to imagine the number of boats that sailed in and out of Restronguet Creek, when Devoran was one of the busiest small ports in the country, but the *West Briton* reports on the weekly movement of shipping can give us a clearer picture of the situation at Point.

POINT, PORT of TRURO, April 29.—Entered inwards, the Restless, Young, from Llanelly; the Elizabeth and Mary, Rees, from Port Talbot; the Gannell, Francis, from Chester; the Susannah, Goss, from Salcombe; and the Merton, Hoskins, from Aberavon.
Cleared outwards, the Blanch, Treweek, for Neath; the Merton, Hoskins, for Swansea; the Gannell, Francis, for Liverpool; the Restless, Young, for Bideford; the Lord Rolle, Samuel, for Llanelly; and the Albert, Griffin, for Port Talbot.

From the *West Briton*, May 1st 1840

To give just three examples of the shipping movements: September 2nd 1848 the paper reported ten ships arriving from South Wales, one from Glasgow and one from Poole in Dorset. Thirteen ships sailed out, twelve for South Wales and one for Newcastle. April 30th 1851 six ships were reported arriving from various ports in Wales and eight ships leaving, four for South Wales, three for Liverpool and one for London. Three years later, on January 26th fifteen ships were reported arriving from Wales and one from Plymouth. If you add to this the number of river boats used for local trade and communication between ship and shore, the scene must have been one of lively movement and change.

Coal, timber, limestone, bricks, lead ore and many other goods would be

28

landed for local use or for transporting further inland, while the quay hutches would be piled high with copper ore, smelted lead and later tin waiting to be loaded on to the barges. This was Cornwall's industrial heyday.

Shipwrecks

There were dangers in this method of transport as the wrecks that litter the coasts of Cornwall show all too clearly. One gale could wreak havoc with ships and lives, as in October 1823 when fourteen ships and nineteen fishing boats were lost, and on another occasion in 1859 when twenty-four ships were wrecked. Nicholas Olive, whose father and elder brother were waterman at Point in 1841, was a tin miner for a short time and then took to the sea. He was living near the Green with his wife and three daughters in 1861, a mariner, who became master of the *Tremenheere,* which foundered on New Year's Day 1875, with the loss of all hands.

The *J.S.T.* built at Carnon Yard in 1858 was lost only six years later off Hartland. Her end was witnessed by Sir George Stucley of Hartland Abbey who wrote, "The sea was very heavy, the wind blowing in strong gusts..... About 12.12 pm a tremendous sea burst with a foaming crest over her..... She shipped two or three seas, holding on until about 12.30 pm when in Hartland Race, about two miles from shore, she fell over on her beam ends, and in one moment all had vanished."

The *Lizzie R Wilce,* built eighteen years later at Carnon Yard, lasted for longer. She was "an elegant clipper-bowed schooner," sailed on many long runs, to the Caribbean for pineapples and sugar, to Newfoundland for fish, to Argentina for phosphates and to South Africa to transport gold mining equipment from Harvey's of Hayle. She was finally wrecked in home waters at St. Ives in 1908.

The Shipping Decline

The slump in mining in the last quarter of the nineteenth century obviously took its toll, and the amount of commercial shipping gradually decreased, but perhaps not as spectacularly as at Devoran, where silting up of the channels became a major problem especially after the gales of 1879. Ships were still an important form of transport for Point, and some people can remember barges (one called *Marian)* being loaded with tin for transferring to larger boats in Falmouth Harbour. Coal boats also continued their trade and barges loaded with road stone landed their cargo on Point Quay.

Nowadays as the tide comes in on summer weekends, small boats tack busily to and fro, outboard engines sputter noisily and colourful sailboards skim effortlessly over the water, all for pleasure. Most of the quay area is now split up into private gardens and slipways, but much of Point Quay remains intact and has recently been bought for the community. For most of the year it is a place for quiet contemplation, watching the tide creep in or studying the now sadly depleted bird population. It is only on Regatta Day that it again hums with noise and activity and as the working boats surge by, sails filled and ropes creaking, we are reminded of the importance of the commercial shipping of the past.

2) ROADS

Hazards

"The roads are so very bad both to Newham, Pill and Point that it is little short of cruelty to drive horses and mules over them."

Walk along the track today between Rope House and Chycoose or the path from Trolver to Harcourt after heavy rain and experience the thick mud and water-filled ruts; then imagine it churned knee-deep by the hooves of laden pack animals as they slipped and slithered in the muck. The road from Point Quay to Carnon Downs would have been like this, as the above extract written in 1797 shows, even though this was a vital link between the mines and the boats.

Until the building of the quay there was no road here. There was just the network of paths and tracks linking one farm with another and the bridge at Penpol probably dates from this earlier time. The tracks then joined up with the two "main" roads running on either side of the area, from Truro to Penryn via Perranwell and the southerly route via the ferries at King Harry and Restronguet Point. These roads were also unsurfaced, muddy and often unfenced on the open downs, such as on Carnon Downs and Feock Downs. Travel was slow, difficult and sometimes dangerous and not something to be undertaken lightly.

Two examples illustrate this, one from each of these "main" roads. In 1754 the Truro-Penryn road over Carnon Downs to Perranwell was described as "so ruinous and bad in winter that (it) cannot...be kept in good repair." An unpleasant accident was recorded on the other route in 1791 at Restronguet. The ferry was transporting several people and three horses when one of the animals took fright in mid-stream capsizing the boat in its terrified struggles. Which was worse for the passengers, the flailing hooves of the horse or being flung into the cold waters?

In the Royal Cornwall Museum in Truro can be seen the massive Trewinnard Coach which belonged to the Hawkins family in the eighteenth century. Its use would have been very limited on Cornwall's appalling roads and in fact comparatively few wheeled vehicles were used at all until the roads became better.

Improvements

As production from the mines rose in the late eighteenth century and Falmouth became an important packet port, so good roads became increasingly vital. Parishes had the responsibility for looking after their own roads, but there had been little incentive to do much beyond the occasional filling in of potholes. Now a more effective system was needed and from the mid-eighteenth century Turnpike Trusts were formed to take responsibility for sections of main roads, charging tolls for their use. Road engineers began to surface, build new bridges and re-route. The improvements could be quite dramatic.   "The road all the way is excellent," wrote a coach traveller in 1795 about the Falmouth - Truro road. And that was before the more drastic improvements undertaken by William McAdam, son of the famous road maker John McAdam, in the 1820s.

The importance of these turnpike roads is perhaps illustrated by this extract from the *Royal Cornwall Gazette*, in July 1863. "Obstruction: William Whitford driver of a timber waggon was fined 30s for allowing his waggon to obstruct the turnpike road near Carnon Gate while he was in the public house drinking." This was a large sum of money then.

However the side roads remained the responsibility of the parish until the end of the century and there were particular difficulties near Point, as this extract from the *West Briton* of May 1st 1840 indicates. "On Tuesday evening last, Mr. Trewhella, clerk to Mr.Knight, brewer in Truro, was returning from Point when his horse fell over a plank projecting in the road in front of the Smelting Works - he was severely injured - but prompt assistance gives hope of recovery. The place is dangerous at any time, but the road having been repaired with slag from the furnaces, its boundaries are very indistinct, and at night the danger is increased by sudden flashes of light when the fire is stirred."

The Feock Vestry Book records in the annual meeting of 1847 that the road from Point to Tregoose was to be kept in good repair. No mention was made about the one in front of the smelter. Another meeting in 1895 has minuted, "Mr. Michell called attention to the state of the road from Penpol to Gunpiper and said that it was not safe for anyone to travel over." It goes on to say that the matter had been brought before the Highways Committee; the County Councils had begun to take over responsibility for roads.

William Michell in his donkey shay
(Courtesy Mr. and Mrs. R. Michell)

31

Foot and Wheel

The inhabitants of Penpol and Point would not have used the roads much to travel to their jobs as people do today. Their work was on their doorstep; the idea of commuting even the four miles or so to Truro was not a necessary option. If they went to church at Feock or later at Devoran most would walk, although some people might have a horse, a pony and trap or a donkey shay. If they wanted to go further afield then walking was often the only way unless a boat could be used. Distances covered on foot would horrify some people today. Even when public transport began, walking could still be a necessity.

In the early 1900s John Trenhaile, farming at Feather Cock Hill (now Hillside Farm), began a twice weekly service to Truro in his horse-drawn wagonette on Wednesdays and Saturdays. This however was of no help to Mrs. Hazel Michell as a girl who had to walk the three miles or so from Point to Perranwell Station every schoolday to catch the train into Truro with the return journey to do again in the evening. On arrival in the town she still had to walk to reach the County School in Strangways Terrace. Her husband had an even longer walk as a boy, because he had to go right across the town to climb the hill on the far side to Truro School.

In the early 1930s John Trenhaile became motorised and the photo below shows his new bus as well as the typical lorries of the time. The increasing dependability and use of motors brought some of the most far-reaching changes in everyday life, but in their earlier days they could cause quite a lot of problems. Mr. Alan Burley, grandson of Edward and Caroline Bath (see section on the Bath Tragedy), recalls that his father had one of the first cars in Cornwall, a DeDion Bouton, which he used to take Richard Bath to his wedding in Truro. The car refused to climb Arch Hill (scene of the earlier Bath tragedy), so in full morning dress they had to push the car all the way up. Perhaps the groom rather than the bride arrived late on this occasion.

John Trenhaile's new motor bus near Point Quay about 1932
(Courtesy Mr. and Mrs. G. Crocker)

32

Road Names

Names given to roads can give hints of the past. The extract earlier from the *West Briton* gives a clue to the naming of Black Road for the now-surfaced bridle track leading from what was Lemon Quay towards Rope House; the slag from the smelters was scattered along here. (Hayle also has its Black Road for the same reason.) Rope House in its turn has given the name Ropewalk to the higher part of the track. Whether this or the path leading past the house was the original ropewalk is not clear. A little bit of social change is illustrated here; the name Black Road is now being superseded by Ropewalk, no doubt because it is thought to give a better image to this now residential area, but it is a pity if the old names are forgotten.

Quarry Hill was the earlier name for Trolver Hill; houses are now built in the hollows where stone was cut probably for the building of the quays and the cottages. Harris's Hill led from the bridge up to the Feock road and Four Turnings. Richard Harris was a carpenter living along here in Rivulet Vale for much of the second half of the nineteenth century. Stamps for crushing ore were working on the site of the later Penpol Boatyard and the short, steep hill leading up from there was known as Stamps Hill. The steep footpath from the Tram Road to Ropewalk is called Stack Lane as the tall chimney of the tin smelter was built at the top. Saltbox Lane leads from the bottom of Point Green to the house of the same name on the Tram Road. The origin of this name is a mystery but salt was a very important commodity for cleaning and preserving and perhaps it was stored here.

The Old Tram Road skirting the northern side of Restronguet Creek from Devoran to Point, provides today a beautiful walk at any season of the year. One hundred and sixty years ago it would have been a treeless tramway, a railway line for horse-drawn waggons.

A granite sett complete with cast-iron "chair" (Devoran)

3) THE REDRUTH AND CHASEWATER RAILWAY

"The first fruits: may the harvest be abundant"

Origin and Opening

A letter written in April 1817 by Alfred Jenkin, agent for the Robartes business concerns, to one of the Welsh smelting companies, highlights how unsatisfactory was the dependence on pack animals especially after a wet season which ruined hay and corn. "Horses and mules have suffered exceedingly from which cause and the extreme badness of the roads we find it very difficult to get ores carried to the wharfs .... upwards of 50 mules have died out of stocks in the Pill district ...... some poor carriers will continue while the present stock of mules last, others talk of selling them and say they will not continue in a losing concern." Less than nine months later John Swan was writing about 300 mules arriving during the night at the new Lemon Quay. (See section on Shipping.)

The numbers of horses and mules used must have been vast as were the problems of feeding them when harvests were bad. What made it worse for the industrialists was the uncertainty of deliveries during the winter months when roads could become impassable quagmires. A more dependable method of transport was desperately needed

In 1819 John Taylor, a successful mining entrepreneur, took over the lease of the Consolidated Mines in Gwennap. He discovered there possibly the biggest copper lode ever found in the world at that time and before many more years had passed he had provided a new, improved transport system, the Redruth and Chasewater Railway. In 1826 "the first true railway in Cornwall" was officially opened.

The Redruth and Chasewater Railway was not the first mineral line to be built in the county, but as with modern trains the wheels of the waggons were flanged rather than the rails. The earlier mineral tramway from Poldice to Portreath on the north coast, started in 1809 and finished by 1819, had flanged rails to take the plain wheels of the waggons. This can be seen today in the Royal Cornwall Museum where there is a section of the rail with the Directors' Carriage, the oldest surviving passenger carriage in the world.

To include "Chasewater" in the name of the railway seems rather odd as the main line ran from Redruth to Devoran, but the branch to Chacewater originally planned was never built because of the falling output from Wheal Busy. (The "spelling mistake" is deliberate because in the official name of the railway "Chasewater" is always spelt with an "s". This was apparently normal at the time the company was formed.)

In the opening ceremony held in January 1826 a banner was carried blazoned with the words, "The first fruits: may the harvest be abundant." For Devoran the harvest was abundant as it became for a time one of the busiest small ports in the country.

The Point Extension

Although Point now became superseded as the main shipping terminus in Restronguet Creek, it did not fade in importance as did the wharfs at Pill Creek and Roundwood Quay, because in 1827 an extension of the line was built along the northern shore of the creek to Point Quay. This created a boom time for Point and its immediate area for the next forty or fifty years. This extension used horse-drawn waggons for the whole of its life even after steam engines were brought into use for the main line in the 1850s.

Although very few people in the area worked on the railway - Richard Webber is recorded as a platelayer in 1881 and Charles Rees Junior as a railway clerk in 1891 - the Point extension increased the number of ships using the quays. A lead smelter was built by Lemon Quay in 1827 and the railway line was extended past Daniell's Quay to incorporate this. This smelter was soon the biggest source of work in the area. Later when the tin smelting works were developed, the line ended where Creek Cottage now stands.

Decline and Closure

The profits of the railway reached a healthy two to three thousand pounds a year peaking at £3,671 in 1845. They then fluctuated below this figure for the next twenty five years, but the figures for 1870 and 1871 illustrate graphically the effect of the sudden slump in copper mining. In 1870 the profits were £1,248 but in 1871 they dropped to £402. This was no temporary decline in fortune as copper mining stopped almost completely and although tin mining continued, it was on a greatly reduced scale.

The railway kept going for another forty-five years but it was against increasing difficulties. Coal continued to be carried as well as tin ore during the short boom times and bricks until the closure of the St. Day Brickworks in 1912. The horse-drawn waggons also took away the roadstone that had been unloaded on the quay, but the use of the railway was then declining rapidly and in the face of growing losses it finally closed in 1915.

The rails were taken up and the course of the track became a muddy "road" full of pot holes. Children walked along it to go to school at Devoran needing rubber boots to get through the huge puddles as Mrs. Iris Dunstan vividly remembers. In the 1950s after some legal wrangling it was finally surfaced to become the beautiful, small road it is today winding beside the creek.

If you are observant you can still see evidence of the railway apart from the sign saying "Old Tram Road". On Point Quay look for the rectangular, granite blocks with two holes in them, almost hidden in the short grass. These are the sleeper blocks to which the rails were fixed by cast iron chairs. A wander around Narobo Creek and Devoran will show similar evidence and some can be seen in the wall leading up to Penpol Farm. The narrowness of the road between Point and Devoran also gives a clue to its origins as it was perfectly suitable for the four-foot railway gauge for which it was built, but today's drivers need to be prepared for some nifty reversing when two cars meet. Although there is so little to see of this line, which lasted for less than ninety years, it provided a vital link for Point and Penpol making possible their own industrial revolution.

CHAPTER THREE

THE LEAD SMELTING WORKS
"a great boon to the neighbourhood"

LEAD AND SILVER

John Taylor, the great mining manager, estimated in 1823 that British mines supplied about two-thirds of the world's consumption of lead. Many mines in Cornwall produced some lead and for a time East Wheal Rose, at the end of what is now the Lappa Valley Miniature Railway, was England's largest lead mine. Lead was in demand for the building industry, ship building and munitions and was also used by pewterers, glassmakers and especially potters for making glazes. Penpol and Point played a part in its production.

John Swan, who had built Lemon Quay, took advantage of the new rail communications to develop the area further. An advertisement in the *West Briton* for September 1827, the same year as the railway was extended to Point, shows that he was not just trading for the great variety of goods needed by the mines, but he had also built a lead smelter at Point close to the quay. However he was unable to reap the benefits as legal wranglings with Lord Falmouth left him

PENPOLL SMELTING WORKS,
RESTRONGUET RIVER.

JOHN SWAN begs to inform the Managers and Proprietors of Lead Mines, in this County, that he is now ready to receive Samples of Lead Ores for Assaying, and to treat for the purchase thereof, on the most favourable terms the state of the Market will allow.

JOHN SWAN has FOR SALE, at *Garras Wharf, Truro,* and at *Lemon* and *Point Quays, Restronguet-River :—*

Swansea, Burry, Neath, and Newport COALS,
Norway and American TIMBER,
Norway and Russia DEALS,
Bar-Iron, Boiler-Plates, Rivet-Iron, Kibble-Plates, and best Charcoal Chain-Iron, Nails, Steel, Miners' Shovels and Hilts.
Rope, Hemp, Tar, Pitch, and Rape Oil,
Miners' Candles and Tallow,
Leather, Engine-Shag and Blanketing,
Lime, Slates, Bridgewater Bricks, Tiles, Laths, &c. &c.

N. B.—Copper Ore shipped with care and dispatch.   Point, Sept. 20, 1827.

LEAD SMELTING WORKS,
Situate at Penpoll, in the Parish of Feock, in which Mr. John Swan lately carried on the Business of a Lead Smelter;

Comprising two Calcining Furnaces, two Flowing Furnaces, three Refining Furnaces, and one Reviving Furnace, with all necessary Working Tools, Test Rings, Moulds, &c. and a stock of Bone Ashes.

These Premises are in complete repair, and in every respect fit for immediate use, and are calculated for Smelting 180 Tons of Lead a month.

Also, all that substantial newly-erected and extensive QUAY, adjoining to the said Lead Works.

36

bankrupt and in 1828 the quay and smelter were up for sale. The public auction notice in the *West Briton* for the new smelting works details eight furnaces for the various processes needed to extract the metal and remove the impurities. The lease was bought by a local partnership which included Robert and William Michell of Truro. The Michell family kept an interest in it until the end as is shown by the leases of 1830, 1852 and 1870, although on a reduced scale in the last years.

Robert Michell had been chief clerk to R.A.Daniell and by this time had built up his own business in partnership with his brother William. They were not only merchants but also had interests in smelting works and mines, such as East Wheal Rose. Taking up the lease of the lead smelter and quay would be a way of consolidating these interests. When Robert died in 1862 sixty men from the lead works walked in the funeral procession.

The lease in 1830 was for twenty-one years at a yearly rent of thirty six pounds. It was to include the lead smelting house, rope house, field, walled garden and the beach or wharf roughly from Stack Lane to where Quay Cottage is today, with use of the road from Rope House to Lemon Quay for carrying lead ore and other materials.

The watercolour painting (see first colour photograph) shows how the works had extended along the creek side by 1857. The huge, square chimney stack on the point is the most obvious feature and although that no longer exists, the retaining wall for the works below still has the flues which led up to it. The height was to reduce the harmful effects of the toxic fumes as the smoke billowed above the fields with their growing crops. This picture gives a distant and rather sanitised view of the smelter; the *West Briton* extract in the previous section on "Roads" gives a more vivid reminder of the dangers lurking at close quarters.

Silver is often found with lead and Cornish lead had the highest average value of silver. An extract from the *West Briton* in July 1838 illustrates this.

" SILVER FROM PENPOLL SMELTING WORKS

A large plate of this valuable metal was taken from the furnaces of Messrs. Michell and Co's lead works at Penpoll near Truro on Tuesday se'nnight. The precise weight of this plate we do not know, but we believe it was about 7,000 ounces. The plate extracted the preceding month weighed between 6 and 7,000 ounces, and we understand that the quantity of silver in its purest state obtained at the works during the last twelve months exceeded 50,000 ounces."

Another account twenty five years later describes the "Penpoll Works" as one of only two lead smelting works in Cornwall at the time. "These works...are capable of manufacturing upwards of 200 tons of lead monthly, occasionally turning out a lump of silver weighing half a ton."

The Workers
This article also gives some details about the work force: "from sixty to a hundred hands are constantly employed at liberal wages, a great boon to the

neighbourhood and fully appreciated by the well-informed and industrious classes." A typical sentiment of the time.

Certainly a high percentage of the men in the area were lead smelters and others must have had work directly connected such as carpenters, coopers and blacksmiths as well as some of those described as "labourers" in the census returns. The same *West Briton* article states that lead, besides coming from Cornish mines, also came sometimes from Aberystwyth, Teignmouth and "occasionally Antwerp." The smelted lead was shipped mainly to London "to which freights are low, rarely exceeding 7/- a ton." This brought work for the porters, watermen and sailors.

Peter Pascoe

There was quite a high turnover of workers, but a few men remained for many years; one of these was Peter Pascoe. He was born in St. Blazey in 1825, the son of William Pascoe, a miner. He began work at the Penpoll Lead Smelting Works when he was about thirteen years old, first of all as a general labourer and then as a lead smelter and refiner. He lodged in the household of James Nettle, one of the managers of the works, who must have thought highly of him to give him the following reference in 1846.

To whom it may concern.

This is to certify that Peter Pascoe has been working upwards of eight years in the Penpoll Lead Smelting Works as Smelter and Refiner, during which time has been found of good Moral Character, honest, industrious and respectful at all times and also a very able working Man.

By this time Peter had been married for nearly three years to Elizabeth Stevens, the daughter of one of his work mates, Mathew Stevens. This teenage bride and groom set up home and over the next twenty-two years produced twelve children. Their eldest daughter, Frances (Fanny), was given the second name of "Nettle": no doubt one of that family acted as a godparent.

During the early 1860s they would have needed all the help that their strong Methodist faith could give them, with the death of their eldest son, aged twenty, as well as four daughters. Then in 1869 Elizabeth died, still only forty-three years old. With four children still at home to be cared for, it was not surprising that Peter married again, his new wife being a dressmaker from Point, Sarah Ann Rees, also from a Methodist family. They had one daughter called after her mother. It was she who told her daughter about going to the corn mill for "seconds." (See section on Corn Mill.)

By the time of Peter's second marriage, the lead works was running down, but he seems to have stayed until the end, surprisingly still being described as a silver refiner in the census for 1881. But ten years later, aged sixty-six, with job opportunities decreasing, he was working in the new tin smelting house as a labourer. So he ended as he began.

The End of the Lead Works

By 1871 the number of people recorded as lead smelters in the immediate area had reduced to only four from a high point of twenty-four in 1851. Cornish lead mining was declining sharply at this time. The price of lead dropped as competition from North America, Australia and Spain increased. By 1881 no lead smelters are recorded, apart fron three retired ones in Chycoose. This is not the end of the smelting story however, because tin smelting in Penpol started up just as lead smelting was finishing.

The tall, square chimney stack remained as a landmark at Point until about 1910 when Mrs. Hazel Michell's father Elijah Searle had it taken down. This happened about five o'clock in the evening just as Mr. Reg Crocker's father, who had been watching for the explosion, had to go to ring the knocking-off bell for the tin works and so he missed what must have been a spectacular collapse. The recycling of material was quite usual then and these bricks can still be seen in the two semi-detached houses Mr. Searle had built just below where the chimney once stood overlooking the quay. His great nephew, Mr. Graham Crocker, is living in one of those houses today.

The tall, square stack of the lead smelting works, date unknown
(Courtesy R.I.C.)

Lead Smelters Lead the Way

The story of the lead smelting works cannot finish without mention of the effect it had on village life. It provided not only work both directly and indirectly for many of the men of the area, but also a school for the children, the Feock Lead Smelting School. (See later section.)

The managers or captains of the lead smelting works lived in Point close to their job in the two parts of Point House. This building has bricks in its structure possibly of the early eighteenth century, so it is almost certainly the oldest house around the Green, although now greatly changed. These managers would have acted as leaders (no pun intended!) in the life of the village. The Nettle family, originating from St. Agnes, came to Point probably some time during the 1830s. James Nettle, who gave Peter Pascoe his reference, was Agent for the works and after his death in 1851, his son, John, also a lead smelter, took over this role. He was living in Point with his young family and his new, improved status is shown by the household acquiring a living-in servant.

Capt. Nettle (like the mine managers the smelting work managers were also given this title) is recorded as subscribing towards the building of the new Wesleyan Chapel in 1861 and two of his sons, Richard and John, became active as Sunday School teachers during the 1860s, but later moved away perhaps at the time of their father's death in 1870.

Humphrey Broad Champion appears for the first time in 1861, described as "Accountant Assayer". He was perhaps no stranger to the village as William Broad Champion, probably his younger brother, was a merchant's clerk lodging with Richard Chellew, sailmaker, in his house on the Green in 1851 shortly before marrying Richard's sister. William's father is recorded in the marriage register as "Mine Agent" and a Captain Champion was manager of East Wheal Rose, so there could be a direct link between Humphrey, the lead mine and the lead smelting works at Point.

Humphrey took a leading part in the Wesleyan Sunday School. The earliest teachers' records show him as being Secretary and one of the Super-intendents in 1866. He was a teacher and in 1868 he had the job of buying the books for rewards for the children and for replenishing the library. Penny Readings were held in support of the library. "Mr. H. B. Champion, the manager, for the opening reading selected a beautiful tale by Mr. John Harris, the Cornish poet, entitled *Nat Moss* which was exceedingly well received. All the other pieces elicited the approval of all concerned. The readings will continue fortnightly."

He obviously enjoyed sailing and took part in a village regatta off the smelting works quay in July 1870. "Some yachts belonging to gentlemen in the vicinity of Point were present amongst which was a splendidly lined dandy belonging to Mr. Champion." *(W.B., July 1870)* He was still in Point in 1871 but some time after that he moved away, presumably at the closing down of the lead works.

CHAPTER FOUR

TIN MINING

The reddish-brown waters of Restronguet and Penpol Creeks were shown in dramatic aerial views on television all over the country in January 1992. Hundreds of years of man's ingenuity in extracting tin from the bowels of the Carnon Valley had ended in what became known locally as the Wheal Jane Disaster. The polluted flood waters from the last local tin mine ensured that this closing chapter in a long history would not be quickly forgotten locally, even if national publicity was short-lived.

The mines of this area have produced large quantities of tin and, more especially in the nineteenth century, vast amounts of copper from a honeycomb of tunnels and caverns deep underground. Much of the ore was transported to Devoran and Point along the railway, but this area had an even more direct connection with mining. While the lead smelting works was busily processing ore from further afield, tin mining was being carried out on the doorstep, immediately under the tidal waters of Restronguet Creek.

Tin Streaming, Skeletons and Gold
Tin streaming goes back to the early Bronze Age when tin was in demand for mixing with copper to make tools and weapons more sophisticated than the finely-shaped flints of neolithic times. Although no archaeological evidence for Phoenician trade has ever been found in Cornwall, there were trade routes across the county from Ireland to Britanny and there were flourishing communities in Cornwall, as evidenced by cliff castles, barrows and fine artefacts, like the ones that can be seen in the Royal Cornwall Museum.

The Carnon Valley was part of this scene. Antler picks and an early Bronze Age axe have been found on the tin-bearing levels in the river, where tin ore had been deposited by water cutting through the ore-bearing rocks higher up the valley, which were then covered by a thick layer of mud. Other evidence of Bronze Age people is scattered over the nearby hill ridges, where the dead were buried in prominent mounds. The most incongruously situated of these barrows today is the one at Carnon Downs, surrounded by bungalows with the curve of a cul-de-sac following the curve of the barrow. The name of the road, Parc an Crug, Field of the Barrow, gives a clue to what lies at the end.

Tinners of the late eighteenth and early nineteenth centuries made some dramatic discoveries when work was being carried out near Devoran. Skeletons and skulls were dug up, some of them perhaps dating back to prehistoric times. One skeleton found in 1823 aroused a lot of interest at the time. It was found underneath carefully placed pieces of wood. "The head and breast were a little raised above the rest of the body. The left arm was extended a little from the side and the piece of elm on that side rested on the hand..........The knees inclined upwards...and the feet were bent back under the top of the thigh bones and rested on the tin ground," so wrote a correspondent to the *West Briton.*

41

It was not only tin and skeletons which they dug up. These tin streamers carried goose quills whose hollow centres were used to keep safe the tiny grains of gold that they might be lucky enough to find. Wedding rings were sometimes made from gold found in this way. One of the largest gold nuggets ever recorded in Cornwall was found here and can now be seen in the Royal Cornwall Museum. It might look small but it was too big for a goose quill.

Streaming was a large scale operation at this time with great earth banks built to keep out the water as the search for tin moved further down river and deeper into the thick layer of alluvial mud. Remains of these can still be seen above and below Devoran. High tides and floods were a constant threat and in 1811 the banks were badly breached. In the 1820s the first mine under the creek was established, with tunnels extending below the mud which was often sixty feet deep. It only lasted a few years but it made a profit and showed that this was a feasible alternative. One wall of its engine house still stands beside the creek at Carnon Mine, reminiscent of a ruined medieval castle.

Mining near Point

These were boom times for Cornwall and fortunes could be made by anyone with money willing to take a risk. When leases were granted for Penpol Farm they invariably carried certain exemptions on minerals. The lease of 1781 states ".... and also excepting all Tin Tin Works Copper and Copper Works and all other Mines Metals and Minerals."

The lease of 1807 went further, as mentioned earlier (see section on Landowners), to include "liberty for Sir William Lemon to erect and make any Engines Stamping Mills and other Edifices upon the said premises for better working and discovery of mines and making ores merchantable."

In 1827 William's son, Sir Charles Lemon, granted a licence to "search and mine for tin, copper and lead ore throughout the tenement of Harkett (Harcourt) and over that part of the Carnon River in the parishes of Feock and Mylor." About eight years later a mine was opened opposite Point.

Carnon Mine

The mine buildings erected at Carnon Yard for this Lower Carnon Mine, were built on land at the eastern junction of Penpol and Restronguet Creeks. Nothing remains there now except a bumpy, overgrown site, but when the tide is ebbing, a low mud bank can be seen emerging in the middle of Restronguet Creek, a constant hazard to the unwary sailor today. On this a small pile of stones and bubbling water shows where an iron-clad shaft was sunk through this man-made island to the tin bearing level and "people worked day and night as ships passed and re-passed overhead." This iron shaft was sunk by piling silt on its covered top until the weight, up to 100 tons, forced it down. The effort and ingenuity shown is amazing, especially when there was no guarantee of a fat profit at the end.

This mine was a techncal success but a financial failure as the price of tin fell. It had made a loss of £16,000 when it closed in 1842.   However while it was in operation it provided work for many local people. In 1836 two hundred and twelve people were working here including two women and sixty-six children. They must have come from quite a wide area as only four men are described as "miners" in the 1841 census for Chycoose, Point and Penpol, including Nicholas Olive as mentioned earlier (see Shipping), but no doubt others were employed there as carpenters, black-smiths and surface labourers.

The sale of mining equipment advertised in September 1842 and six months later in 1843, gives some idea of the surface work involved. Besides a forty inch pumping engine, there was a smaller sixteen inch rotary one, probably for working the three-headed stamps for crushing the ore, there were two horse whims presumably to wind the ore up to the surface, several buddles to separate the crushed ore from waste matter by passing it through water, iron kibbles for carrying the ore to the surface and boats no doubt used to reach the shaft on the island.

The Restronguet Creek Tin Stream Company

How would people react today if a tin mine was opened below Point Green, with a tall engine house partly blocking the view of the creek, with tram waggons trundling over wooden staging, stamps thumping and piles of tin and coal heaped up on the foreshore? The outcry against it would no doubt be greater than ten years or so ago, when the suggestion was made to dredge the creek for its tin deposits, because it would not even help the sailing fraternity by deepening the channel.

One hundred and twenty years ago there was such a mine below the village. The painting (see colour section) is no figment of the imagination but a painstaking representation of the mine workings with the cottages of the Green clearly recognisable in the background. It was begun in 1871 and ended in 1874, spanning the time of a small boom in the tin markets, and it would probably have been welcomed by local people for providing work at a time when the lead works were running down and the tin works were not yet at full production.

Much more is known about this mine than the earlier one at Carnon Yard, because there were regular articles in the Mining Journal and one of the managers, Charles Taylor, gave a report about it to the Penzance Institution of Mechanical Engineers. He was the grandson of John Taylor, the developer of mines in the Gwennap area.

The Making of the Mine

The wooden staging shown in the painting carries the winding head gear over Taylor's Shaft, the main shaft 108 feet deep. This was sunk below high tide level perhaps for two reasons: it reduced the distance of the levels underground and it avoided the payment of dues to Lord Falmouth, the landowner with mineral rights above high water level.

A deep level was then driven out under the creek nine feet high and five feet wide. This large cross-cut carried a tramroad raised two and a half feet above the level of the bottom to provide a reservoir to collect water seeping in without interfering with the transportation. In fact the water problem was less than feared, the worst leakages being close to shore rather than in the middle of the creek.

The next stage in the operation aroused a lot of interest as it was the sinking of a second shaft, Charles Shaft, through the mud in the middle of the creek to provide better ventilation. A different and less laborious method was used for sinking this shaft than the earlier one at Carnon Yard, although the amount of time and effort still involved shows the confidence of these adventurers.

Wooden staging was first driven into the soft mud and then cast iron cylinders, each one weighing two and a half tons, were lowered by crane onto the staging. The first one was sharpened on the bottom edge and acted as a knife, slicing deep into the silt with the weight of the next one on top. The mud was then cleared out of the middle and the next cylinder was positioned over the top and attached to stone-filled barges. As the tide ebbed so these barges settled deeper into the water and then onto the mud, forcing the cylinders down further. The core of mud was then cleared out again ready for the next section. In this way a shaft 78 feet deep was driven down to the bed rock which was then linked up with the deep level.

Only then after all this labour, could parallel levels be cut through the tin bed further out into the creek. Unlike many of the mines in hard rock, all the levels had to be strongly timbered with eight inch Norway balks every two and a half feet, capped by ten inch balks. Not until much of this had been done could the extraction of tin really get under way.

Mechanisation

It is difficult to know how many people from the Point-Penpol area were employed here because it had scarcely started at the time of the 1871 census, when only three miners are mentioned, one man at Chycoose and two at Trolver. By the time the next census was taken the mine had closed down. When it was fully operational by the middle of 1873 it employed 28 men and 14 boys underground with 16 men and 9 boys on the surface, far fewer than the previous mine.

One of the reasons for the reduced numbers would have been the greater use of mechanisation. In the picture a man can be seen pushing a tram from the head of the shaft along the staging to the processing area. "This was the first instance in Cornwall where the stuff broken in the mine was drawn through a perpendicular shaft to the surface in the same trams which carried it along the levels to the shaft," so said Richard Taylor, Charles' father, at the meeting in Penzance. The mine also had the first mechanical jiggers used in the county. These were power-operated shaking frames which separated the heavier tin from the mud when water was washed over them.

The heaps in the foreground of the picture show coarser waste material on the left piled on the quay ready to be used as ballast for the boats. The heap on the right is of finer material, which has probably been brought from the stamps by the chute above it. Alluvial tin needed very little stamping for crushing it, so there was only a small two-headed stamps on the site, unlike some other mines with their monster machines. At the Levant mine near St. Just, the stamps were enlarged to ninety-six heads and could sometimes be heard as far away as Penzance.

The engine house with its smoking chimney and powerful machinery must have been a very conspicuous feature both from land and water. It pumped water from the mine; the black rising main in the shaft that brought the water to the surface can be seen under the headgear, with the flat rods that connected the engine with the pump running under the staging. It was probably this same water that was used in dressing the tin as it would have been the most convenient source. The twin fly wheels on the engine show that it probably powered the stamps as well, and it would also have drawn the trams up the shaft.

When the ore had been stamped, graded, washed on the frame and in a buddle it was ready for the smelting house and the most convenient one would be the new Penpoll Tin Smelting Works a hundred yards or so along the tramway beside Penpol Creek. However as the mine was situated right by the quay it might have been bagged, weighed - the scales are in the foreground - and loaded on a boat to be taken to one of the other smelting houses perhaps in Truro. It would all depend on the best price being offered.

The End of Mining
Money as always was the vital factor and by 1873 the mini tin boom was over. Australian tin was more prolific, cheaper and in many cases purer. The Restronguet Creek Tin Works soon joined the ranks of the abandoned mines. The *Royal Cornwall Gazette* carried a small item on March 21st 1874. "The Restronguet Mine, near Truro, has been stopped. The men commenced to pull up the materials last week."

It was a surprisingly long time before there was a public auction. Perhaps the managers were hoping for a revival. If they did they were to be disappointed. Any lingering hopes were dashed by the continued low price, and the deaths in 1876 first of Captain Robert Ford, the assistant manager, and then six months later of Charles Taylor.

In 1879 the sale was finally advertised. It included the stamps, pumps, balance and angle bobs and the huge amount of paraphernalia needed such as rod pins, kibbles, shaft cage, smith's bellows, scrap iron, timber and the usual account house furniture.

Today there is little to remind us of this interesting mine. At low tide the remains of the iron shaft can be seen poking up through the mud and in the orchard near the lime kiln, the lower part of the retaining wall shows some evidence of the foundations of the engine house. The rest has gone or is effectively hidden. It is believed that trams laden with ore are still below the creek, left just as they were when the mine was abandoned.

RESTRONGUET TIN STREAM COMPANY
(Limited),
POINT, DEVORAN

M R W. T. DAVEY (Auctioneer, &c, Redruth), has been favored with instructions to SELL (without reserve), at PUBLIC AUCTION, on TUESDAY the 15th day of April next, commencing at One o' clock precisely, at the above Mine, the undermentioned MATERIALS, & c.,
1 new (Husband's Patent) 2 head PNEUMATIC STAMPS, with shafts and fly-wheel, 9 16 in. PUMPS, WINDBORE, DOOR PIECE, &c., 2 15-inch PLUNGER POLES with Stocking, 1 20-ft. DRY TUBE, BALANCE and ANGLE BOBS (complete), 5 cast iron CYLINDERS, 6-ft. diameter forming 5 fms of tubbing for a shaft, winch, strapping plates, staples and glands, rod pins, sundry blocks, chain, tram wagons, cog and other wheels, kibbles, saddles, circular riddle, screw tools, brass and iron weights, smith's bellows, smiths and niners' tools, shaft cage, wheel-barrows, cross-cut and hand (?) saws, ladders, pitch pine 12-in. rod, 7-in. launders, boat, tin hutches, scrap iron, a lot of old and useful timber, and sundry other articles in use in mines, including an excellent miner's theodolite (by Wilton), also the ACCOUNT HOUSE FURNITURE.
MARK SALE, "At Restronguet, Point, Devoran," on Tuesday the 15th April, 1879, at 1 o'clock precisely.
A conveyance will leave Perranwell Railway Station for the mine, on the day of Sale, on the arrival of the 12.7 a.m. down train, and will return in time to meet the 4.55 up train.
Dated Salem House, Scorrier, April 1st, 1879.

Transcribed from the *Royal Cornwall Gazette*, 4th April 1879

46

CHAPTER FIVE

THE TIN SMELTING WORKS
"To see the red hot slag run out was one of the highlights for us."

The Rise and Fall

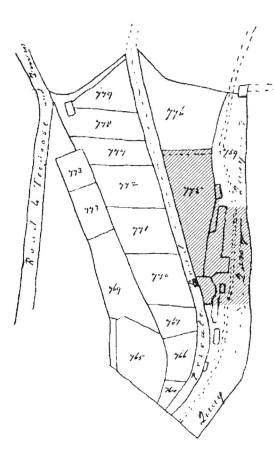

The tin smelter was still working in living memory, not closing until after the first World War in 1921. It began in 1870 when a lease was drawn up between Colonel Tremayne, the heir to Sir Charles Lemon, and London metal brokers William Shakespeare, Henry James and Kenneth Haweis James. The plan accompanying the lease shows that it was only the middle part of the land involved from earlier leases, so presumably the lead works were still operating, but the Ordnance Survey Map of 1878 shows that tin smelting

Map for the lease of the new tin smelting works 1870. (C.R.O. WH 1498/2)
Reproduced by permission of Cornwall County Record Office: copyright reserved.

works were established both by Lemon Quay and higher up Penpol Creek. A new lease drawn up in 1880 between Colonel Tremayne and William Teague for the London based Penpoll Tin Smelting Company confirms this expansion as it covers all the land from the original leases including the bone mill and pond right up to Penpol Bridge.

A new, tall chimney was built on the higher land above, at the top of Stack Lane, with long flues going through the retaining wall underground, to join a larger flue built alongside Black Road. This collected arsenic deposits, and after the works closed Fred Morcom was given a three month agreement "to carry away and sell arsenic soot or crude arsenic from the disused arsenic flues and chambers." These flues go underneath and edge our garden today but so far we are suffering no noticeable hair loss from eating our garden produce.

Although copper mining failed spectacularly in the early 1870s because of "bottoming out", increased deep mining costs and overseas competition, tin extraction continued although at a reduced rate with mini booms in the 1870s, and early twentieth century. However the increasing production from mines in Bolivia and Nigeria reduced the importance of Cornish tin so the Penpoll Tin Smelting Company set up a subsidiary smelting works on the Mersey, as Liverpool was the main port for the imported ore. This soon became the chief smelter for the company and in 1921 the Cornish works were closed down, although the name was kept for a few more years.

Smelting and Smelters
If the census returns are an accurate guide, fewer men were employed than in the heyday of the lead smelter. In 1871 Point with the Rope House tenements had eight tin smelters, there was one each in Penpol and Trolver and Chycoose had two smelters without specifying whether they were tin or lead. In 1881 there were only three in the area and in the last available census of 1891 there were six including Thomas Crocker. There were of course the other occupations connected with the works. Mr. Reg Crocker can remember the cooper called Davey, who made barrels near the foreshore by the cottage, Waters Edge. These were used for storing strips of tin.

Houses have been built where the works once stood. At the bottom of Black Road (Ropewalk), where the new house Tregunna now stands, was the stables. Creek House was originally the offices and the railway terminated just beyond. Remains found in the garden also show that the crucible house was near here. Then came a large tin storing shed where the flats are now built and beyond this was the main part of the smelting works at Polmarion.

Mr. Reg Crocker can remember four square furnaces, each with their own name such as Old Slagger. These furnaces were lined with clay brought by the horse tram. He used to help his father load the tin ore, like brown sandy gravel, into a furnace. The hole was then stopped with clay while the furnace was heated. When the ore had melted, a long iron rod with a square end was rammed in and turned to break through the clay bungs on each side to let the molten ore flow out into a large container. It was then poured into moulds where the lamb and flag stamps were floated on top to mark the ingots. Each smelting company had their own stamp and the lamb and flag symbol used by the Penpoll Tin Company was not unusual. The ore was then loaded on to barges by a crane from the nearby quay to transfer onto sea-going ships in Falmouth Harbour.

48

The working tin smelter after 1910
The lead smelter stack has been demolished.
(Courtesy Mr. and Mrs. R. Michell)

There is still a small buddle by the quayside of Polmarion where tin was processed. This is a circular brick-lined depression where tin ore was mixed with water which carried off the lighter impurities. Stamps, possibly three-headed ones, for crushing the ore worked nearby using water power. These were first set up across the creek where the small stream, which was controlled by sluice gates, comes down on to the beach. Later the water was brought by pipe across the creek to be closer to the site; the end of the pipe is still sticking up near the foreshore. The cottage, Waters Edge, once housed an oil-fired engine perhaps to generate electricity. The foreshore area near the bottom of Stack Lane was the ash pit and clinker from the furnaces was spread on the road, and on the foreshore where it can still be seen.

Miss Marion Chegwyn, a fourth generation inhabitant of Penpol, wrote down in the early 1970s her memories as a child. "The Penpoll Tin Smelting Works was in full working when I was a child and the men worked in shifts, three shifts I am told with twelve to fifteen men in a shift. The ore was brought by rail from Redruth to Devoran and from Devoran to Penpoll in horse-drawn tram waggons. Large coal boats used to come to the Works Quay and unload there and tin was loaded onto Mr. Opie's barge *Marian.* The slag was broken up and shipped to Bristol to make bottles. To see the red hot slag run out into a huge dishlike place was one of the highlights for us and I've had many a scolding for rushing off to see it at night. Another attraction to us as children was the blacksmith's shop belonging to the works."

Penpol House, with its older, large walled garden mentioned in some of the early leases, was built for the managers of the works. Captain Joseph Blight

49

was probably living there with his wife and young children in 1881. Like previous captains he and his family were active in the life of the chapel. He taught at the Sunday School, which his son and four daughters attended regularly once they were old enough. He died in 1891 and his family moved away some time later.

Thomas Teague, presumably related to William Teague who signed the contract in 1880, was another captain of the tin works, living first in Truro, but after Blight's death, moving to Penpol. In the last years Mr. Laity and Joseph Pollard, whose daughters taught in the Sunday School, were managers.

The End of an Era
The tall, round stack was a reminder of these days for some time longer, but in the early 1930s it was brought down, and like its lead works predecessor the bricks were re-used, and the bungalow nearby was built. Observant eyes might recognise its rounded base, now used to store grass cuttings. This was the last obvious symbol of the part played by Penpol and Point in Cornwall's important industrial past.

Workers outside the Penpoll Tin Smelting Works
Frederick Bryant is holding the largest shovel, and his brother John Charles
is the fifth to his right.   (Courtesy of Mr. R. Bird)

50

CHAPTER SIX

SHIPBUILDING

The Rhoda Mary

"A new clipper schooner has been launched from the shipbuilding yard of Mr. John Stephens, St. Feock, near Truro. A large concourse of people collected in that picturesque part of the River Fal, Restronguet Creek, and the launch was eminently successful."

According to one story the bottle refused to break at this launching, and as the boat moved off down the slip, John Stephens' fifteen-year-old son, John, went racing after her and managed to smash it before she reached the water. The *Royal Cornwall Gazette* article continues:

"She was christened the *Rhoda Mary* by a niece of the commander and principal owner Capt. John Meyrick and is destined for the Baltic trade for which according to competent judges she is eminently suitable."

No mention is made of William Ferris, John Stephens' foreman, the designer and builder of this 130 ton ship, one of the most highly regarded shipbuilders of the time, and of all his ships this one, the *Rhoda Mary,* was considered his best.

A fine model of this schooner can be seen in the Maritime Museum on Cotehele Quay by the River Tamar (see colour section) and another one graces the office of William's great-grandson, Mr. Brian Ferris. She was built as a two-masted schooner - later converted to three masts - 101 feet long, with flaring bows and a beam of 22 feet. This narrow width shows that she was built for speed and she soon gained the reputation for being the fastest schooner in operation. Brian Ferris has been told that William based the design on his study of dolphins and mackerel renowned for their sleek speed.

This swiftness was shown on many occasions, such as the time when she left South Shields with a small fleet of other schooners laden with coal for Plymouth. She outstripped her companions so decisively that she had arrived and unloaded her cargo before any of the others had appeared. Over the following years she sailed not only the North Sea, but also the Baltic and Mediterranean, as well as the coastal waters nearer home, making many voyages a year. Unlike some other fine boats she was not destroyed by storms, but time can have just as bad an effect, and she is now a mouldering wreck beside the River Medway.

William Ferris and the Ferris Family
There was one other ship which could rival her for speed and this was the *Katy Cluett* of Fowey.　They only sailed together once and on that occasion
51

the *Rhoda Mary* proved the faster, but whichever won, the Ferris family had proved their ability, because the Fowey ship had been built by William's elder brother, Peter.

William and Peter were not the only shipbuilders in the family: two other brothers, their father, Thomas, their grandfather, Peter, and probably more remote ancestors had all become skilled in this craft (excuse the pun!), building on local beaches such as Pill and Carnon Yard. Boat building of some sort must have been carried on around the creek since people first settled here, both for fishing and for transport, but little detail is known about before the nineteenth century when the name of Ferris dominated the scene.

As industrial production rose during the nineteenth century so the demand for ships increased to transport the goods, and the Ferris family responded to this. It is impossible to tell exactly how many ships were built because those used solely on the Fal and its estuary did not have to be registered and the builders are not always recorded. A few are known built by Peter, the grandfather, all under 50 tons, including a barge in 1819 called *William and Thomas,* the names of his two sons. They probably built the schooner, the *Two Brothers,* in 1836 and Thomas went on to produce a series of schooners in the 1850s with his own sons taking an increasing part.

The size of these boats is noticeably larger: only two under 50 tons, and several over 100 tons, including the *William and Henry.* This was built for the Devoran partnership of Tregoning and Sampson, a schooner of 102 tons, mentioned in a letter by William Tregoning to his father John Simmons Tregoning, when he took his twelve-year-old son to see it being built. "I send you by this post a letter addressed to you by Little John who is quite well and happy. He is here (at Bissoe) again today and I purpose taking him down to Restronguet to see our new ship this evening." Four years later the *J.S.T.* was built, named after William's father. This was an even larger schooner of 127 tons, which as previously mentioned (see section on Shipping) was destined for only a short life as she was wrecked in heavy seas off Hartland Point with the loss of the captain and the six crew.

Thomas Ferris was a better craftsman than businessman.

These larger vessels required greater outlay of capital and by 1858, when the *J.S.T.* was launched, Thomas was owing more to the timber merchants than he could pay and he was declared bankrupt. A few years later his eldest son, Peter, moved to Charlestown, but the three younger ones remained in the area, all as shipwrights. William was appointed as headman for John Stephens, who bought Carnon Yard when Thomas Ferris was forced to sell up, and it was here he built some of his best boats including the *Rhoda Mary.*

William "Foreman" Ferris continued building boats, although on a smaller scale, even after John Stephens sold Carnon Yard in 1880. In Basil Greenhill's book, "The Merchant Schooners," he is described as a "quiet, steady man possessed of a great genius for the use of tools and for the rightness of the feel and shape of those things which he made with them." His last boat was a punt, the appropriately named *Grannie and Grandpa.* He and his wife Joanna, daughter of a Feock carpenter, had at least eleven children, and no doubt they were grandparents many times over. One of his granddaughters, Mrs. Hetty Trebilcock, has a hazy memory of an old man with a big beard who would say to her, "Well, little woman." He died at the age of eighty-seven as he was sitting, pipe in hand, quietly talking. His great-great-great-granddaughter is called Harriet, the name of the very first boat he built.

The Harriet at Point Quay, possibly the first boat built by William Ferris
(Courtesy Mr. C. Warren)

John Stephens at Carnon Yard

John Stephens came from a large Chycoose family who were mainly carpenters and lead smelters. But boats and the sea must have been in their blood, because his brother Hugh built boats at Devoran in the 1860s and another brother, Richard, became a master mariner. John at first followed in his father's footsteps as a carpenter, but in 1858 he bought the Carnon Shipyard, and so began his career as a shipbuilder.

In the first few years he stayed in Chycoose, no doubt getting to

John Stephens about 1880 (Courtesy Capt. G. Hogg)

his yard by boat or, if the tide was too low, by walking or riding through Point and Penpol. The 1861 census shows him at Chycoose Creek, living with his wife, Mary, their five young children and a living-in servant. There was quite a "Stephens" enclave there with two of his brothers and their families and two unmarried sisters living next to each other. Later he moved with his family across the water to Trolver, or Bathtown as it was still called.

On the 3rd inst., Mr. John Stevens launched from his shipbuilding yard, at Carnon, Feock, a fine three-mast brigantine of the following dimensions : Length 102, breadth 32, depth 12 feet; about 280 tons burthen, and classed ten years English Lloyd's. The vessel was named Lizzie R. Wilce by Mrs. Wilce, wife of the master, Capt. E. Wilce, and is owned by him and others, and intended for the foreign trade. After the launch the owners and workmen returned to the moulding loft, where they sat down to a good substantial supper.

(September 1876)

He was not a shipwright so he probably acted more as an administrator than as a builder. The yard seems to have prospered under his direction with an average of at least one ship a year being produced. The midship section for one of the vessels, *Gleaner,* can be seen in the Royal Cornwall Museum as well as details of the largest of all the ships built here, the *Lizzie R Wilce,* one hundred and sixty-two tons. For many years she traded out of Falmouth for fruit and on

54

more than one occasion earned a merchant's bonus for the fastest passage of the season. (See section on Shipping for her end.)

He sold the yard in 1880, the property being "admirably suited for carrying on a shipwright's business," as the sale notice stated. His great-grandson, Captain George Hogg, has researched meticulously into the ship building in the area and has shown that he built at least twenty vessels during the years 1859 to 1879.

Hitchens' Boatyard

By this time the age of large sailing ships was nearly over, as steam ships were "butting through the Channel" more and more frequently. However Carnon Yard continued to produce boats although on a smaller scale. There was another prolific boatbuilding family in the area, the Hitchens. ".....There was a host of Hitchens up there in those days....." says Jimmy Morrison in *Living History Under Sail.*

Frank Hitchens was already building working boats in his walled boatyard, set back from the beach at Carnon Yard, while the Stephens' yard was still in operation. He probably took over Stephens' premises when they were sold in 1880. He was about the same age as William Ferris and they were reputedly great rivals, although he has also been described as a pupil of William's. His boats certainly had a reputation for speed so perhaps he did learn some techniques from him.

At least three of the boats he built can still be seen locally. *Royal Oak,* or *Victory* as she is called now, races in the summer regattas with her distinctive red and yellow topsail; *Softwing,* possibly built by Frank's son Tom, has been described as "a perfect example of a dredging boat," and is used by the Cornish Friends of the Maritime Trust; *Shadow,* built for Frank's sons Tom and William, held the record for the Fowey to Falmouth passage race for many years and is still regularly used for oyster dredging by her owner Mr. Frank Vinnicombe. Possibly the two fastest boats Frank built were *Mabel* and the *Evelyn.* (See section on Fishing and the photograph on page 74.)

Tom Hitchens continued to build at Carnon Yard, mainly small skiffs and oyster dredging punts such as *Maid Nancy* and *Flip Flap,* which were used for popular rowing races between Chycoose and Devoran. He was probably the last boat builder at Carnon Yard.

Standing on the sheltered, curved beach today it is difficult to imagine the noise and bustle a hundred years or so ago. Now there are just the cries of birds or the excited bark of a dog taking its owner for a walk. At least in the summer there is small-boat activity, but no longer the sound of hammering echoing over the water, the hiss of the saws from the sawpit or the clip clop of horses dragging the long trunks down to the shore. There is no ribbed silhouette of a hundred-ton boat to be seen standing on the stocks. If you look carefully you can just make out the broken stakes of the wooden jetty that once jutted out over the beach towards the creek, but little else survives.

55

Ropes and Sails

Penpol has its "Rope House" and "Rope Walk" so probably ropes were made here at one time, although I have not been able to discover much about this. But where there was shipbuilding there was likely to be rope making somewhere in the vicinity. However there was definitely a sail maker in the area. Richard Chellew, eldest son of the Point customs officer, was practising as a sailmaker in 1841, when he was about twenty years old. He was living next door to his parents on the Green, and the Tithe Map of 1842 shows a sail loft beside the Chellew property. Some years later he moved across the creek to Harcourt, where he was still working in 1881. This would have been closer to the main shipbuilding activity at Carnon Yard and Pill Creek.

(The Falmouth Maritime Museum has descriptive details about rope and sail making methods. It also has a clear guide to the different types of rigging for schooners, ketches, brigs etc. as well as a host of information on other aspects of maritime history in the area.)

Penpol Boatyard

A small boat-repair yard was started before the Second World War beside the beach below Trolver Farm, and this was developed into a bigger concern after the war by Lionel Hicks and his brother, who came from the Scillies. In 1960 Mr. Bob Pizey bought the yard and continued repair work as well as building a small number of wooden boats. Later came the pre-fabricated fibreglass hulls which were then properly fitted out, and this work was continued when Mr. Fox took over the yard in 1978. The smooth, shining woodwork and gleaming brass on these boats must have pleased the eye of many passers-by. But within ten years the business had moved to Penryn and a great tradition seems finally to have come to an end.

For some years old boats were used to act as a breakwater by the beach. These included concrete barges which, I have been told, had been kept in the Percuil River as water barges in case of a nuclear attack. Recent attempts to build houses here have been stopped by a planning decision to keep this access to the water open for commercial use. So perhaps once again streamlined boats could be made and launched here.

Tradition dies hard and the sound of sawing and hammering can still be heard by the creek and tree trunks can still be sometimes seen soaking by the shore. At Carnon Mine, where the Stephens family bought property in the 1850s, Ralph Bird, a descendant of Hugh Eddy Stephens, has revived interest in pilot gigs, those long, sleek rowing boats which used to race each other to gain the custom of the ocean-going sailing ships as they made their way towards harbour. He has built several fine gigs and Devoran, which used to have a gig called the *Fear Not,* has one once again. At the moment he is building one for Hayle. Gig racing, which had almost died out, is once again drawing the crowds on summer evenings as rival teams are urged on to victory.

Looking across Penpol Creek from Trolver to the lead-smelting works. Lemon Quay was below the lead-smelter stack, and Daniell's (Point) Quay just around the corner. (From a watercolour dated 1857, courtesy of the R.I.C.)

The Tin Mine at Point 1874. From an oil painting by T. May, now hanging in the recently refurbished Rashleigh Gallery of the Royal Cornwall Museum. (Courtesy of the R.I.C.)

Point Green 1889. From an oil painting by Charles Rees, a few years after the family's return from Scotland (Courtesy Mr D. Rees)

Chycoose, overlooking Restronguet Creek, a settlement of smallholders in 1842.

Tregoose Farmhouse. John Michell, farmer in 1851, displayed corn seeds at the Great Exhibition.

The model of the **Rhoda Mary** *at the Maritime Museum, Cotehele Quay.*
(Courtesy of the Maritime Museum, Greenwich)

Penpoll Methodist Chapel before the recent refurbishment.
(Courtesy Mr and Mrs G. Crocker)

Winter: The falling tide shows the emergence of the Mine Bank in the distance on the right. The Lower Carnon Mine buildings were near the point on the left. Carnon Boatyard was just beyond.

Spring: Bulb field above the Penpol Valley. Restronguet Creek and Carrick Roads in the distance.

Summer: Penpol and Point Regatta, 1983. A Falmouth Working Boat in the foreground.

Autumn by Penpol Creek, with boats being laid up for the winter.

The memorial windows for Elizabeth and William Chellew in Feock Church.

64

CHAPTER SEVEN

FISHING

"Nobody ever made a fortune oyster fishing but it's been marvellous steady work for a large number of families around the Fal."

Fishing the waters of the Fal must be at least as old as farming the land around it, but for many it has been a spare-time, leisure activity, or at the most a part-time occupation. Around Penpol and Point there were very few men fishing as a main occupation, especially when there was a larger choice of jobs on offer; those that are recorded are usually described as "oyster dredgers." The methods of fishing they used then are still in use today.

The Restronguet Creek Oyster Dredgers, as they were once called, are the world's last oyster boats using only sails or oars. They work the oyster beds in Carrick Roads using triangular iron dredgers that are dragged along the bottom as the boat is allowed to drift. This might seem inefficient but the fishermen agreed in the past not to use powered boats. This was not a quaint refusal to move with the times but a hard-headed realisation that stocks would last no other way. Oyster fishing has now died out on the east coast of England, but in Fal today the quality and quantity are as good as they have been for fifty years according to Mr. Frank Vinnicombe, a fisherman of many years' experience.

About eighteen boats have been fishing regularly during the winter of 1992-3, far fewer than the fifty sailing boats and eighty-seven punts in use in 1925. Mr. Frank Cock, who was born in Point in 1905, was fishing at this time and recalls how hazardous it could be for the larger sail boats to weave their way amongst the punts. A morning's work could bring in 3,500 oysters, but their price was not high, perhaps from 2s 6d to 5s for a thousand. This bears out the quotation at the beginning, made by Mr. Henry Merrifield of Feock, who has had many years experience of oyster fishing.

The number of boats working in the mid-twenties was exceptional; they have always fluctuated according to stocks and the state of the job market. There were many men in the earlier part of this century who worked the oyster beds during the winter season and then found other work in the summer, perhaps on farms or crewing on private yachts.

In the nineteenth century the largest number recorded as fisherman in the census returns was in 1891, at a time when mining, smelting and shipping were all on the decline. In Point there were the young brothers, John and James Abbot, who lived just above the quay, at Rope House there was Thomas Colliver, and across the creek at Trolver were the Hitchens family, boatbuilders but also fishermen. The brothers, William, Tom and James, had the advantage of their father's boat-building skills. In 1886 he built *Shadow* for William and Tom, "very fast and a popular winner at all the local regattas." and in 1896 came *Evelyn,* possibly the fastest boat of its type ever to be built.

Today the Falmouth Working Boats are used mainly for pleasure and their beauty under full sail can be appreciated in the summer regattas, delighting everyone with their power and grace. They can perhaps be seen at their best at the Point and Penpol Regatta, where they manoeuvre in the restricted waters with great skill, surging past the quay only a few feet away from the spectators. Some, like *Victory*, could be returning to the area where they were first built but *Shadow* is not amongst them; she is still a real working boat, laid up for the summer waiting for the start of the new oyster season.

Oyster dredging - photograph by Frank Gibson   (Courtesy Mr. R. Bird)

MARKET GARDENING

A pony trotting along beside the creek drawing behind it a small waggon filled with colourful bunches of flowers, sticks of rhubarb, sacks of potatoes and great white heads of cauliflower or broccoli: this could be the scene when the Hitchens brothers took their produce into Truro or when Harold Bersey set off soon after dawn to sell his produce in Falmouth. By the 1930s the lower slopes of the hills on either side of Penpol Creek were a patchwork of hedges protecting the small fields, full of flowers and vegetables, against the strong south-westerlies that occasionally came roaring up the creek.

It was Harold Bersey's grandfather, Samuel, who had pioneered commercial gardening in the area sixty years or so earlier. He was a smelter in the lead works for much of his life, his family having moved to Point from the Helford area. When Henry Bath built cottages on his land at Trolver in the 1840s the Bersey family moved across the water, and it was here that Samuel began gardening in his later years when the lead works was running down.

Brunel's bridge across the River Tamar, opened by Prince Albert in 1859, made market gardening a commercial proposition in Cornwall. For the first time it became possible to transport perishable goods all the way to London, and Cornwall's mild climate was ideal for the development of early crops. Over the following years London homes were sweetened by Cornish violets and brightened by Cornish daffodils bought from Covent Garden.

Samuel, and later his son Alexander, had no real rivals in the area for many years. But in the late 1920s other businesses began and by 1939 there were seven flower growers on either side of the creek. With the decline in boat building and oyster fishing the Hitchens brothers, Richard, Frank and Dan, developed the small fields bordering Black Road, and the pittosporum hedges still to be seen here are a reminder that they possibly were the first to grow and market it on a commercial scale. But they grew and sold much more besides: violets, anemones, daffodils, narcissi, apples, gooseberries, winter rhubarb, potatoes - the list is almost endless. Shopkeepers placed regular orders, the pony waggon was used for door-to-door sales in Truro and many local people came to buy. One man, disabled by a wound from the First World War, walked with his wife every week from Carharrack to buy produce from the Hitchens' nurseries.

Thousands of anemones and violets were planted each year around the creek. This back-breaking work was followed in due course by picking, when nimble fingers were needed to bunch the flowers, 25 violets to a bunch enclosed in a heart-shaped leaf of winter heliotrope, known locally as coltsfoot. During the Second World War food was at a premium, so all the market gardens had to "dig for victory" and go over to vegetable production. The occasional bunches of violets still found their way to war-torn London as well as the scented, lilac heliotrope flowers. These still bloom in the winter beside Ropewalk.

Experiments were made with miniature daffodils and narcissi by Mr. Grey in the post-war years on his land at the far end of Ropewalk, but the days of these small market gardens were numbered. House building became more profitable than flowers and gradually "desirable residences" grew up instead.

Today bulbs are grown on a larger scale as a farm crop, and even on a dull spring day the hillsides around Penpol and Tregoose can be bright with the glow of thousands of daffodils. Bunches of flowers by a gateway above the Green indicate the second generation revival of the Warren nurseries but the pony waggons have long gone.

Market Gardening at Point and Penpol in the 1940s
This view is looking from Trolver.   *(Courtesy Mrs. N. Hibbert)*

CHAPTER NINE

MIGRATION AND EMIGRATION

Some individuals and families came to live in Point and Penpol but others disappeared. Where did they go? Some moved just a mile or so away, some crossed the Tamar into Devon and beyond, some went to Wales where there were strong connections with Cornwall, and some went even further afield to Scotland. Some left for ever; a few returned. One couple who moved to New Cummock in Ayrshire but returned about eleven years later were Charles Rees and his wife Matilda.

They were married in 1871 and left almost immediately for the north. For some years coal mine managers in Scotland had been looking for skilled Cornish labour, as this *West Briton* extract of 1866 shows. "During the last fortnight, Messrs. Brown and Howatson, from Glasgow, representing the coal and iron masters of that city, have been engaging miners to proceed to Scotland, and already 300 have contracted. The liberal terms offered viz. 4s a day, certain for 12 months, and free transit, have proved attractive."

Charles was a mason not a miner, but he responded to this demand possibly because of the low wages and declining job prospects in Cornwall. A letter he wrote to his older sister, Sarah, and her husband, Peter Pascoe, soon after arrival, gives a number of interesting details. They went first to Bristol, where they were met and entertained by Richard Hockin(g) and his wife, probably the son of Point's limeburner - yet another example of the younger generation moving away. He does not say anything more about the journey, which was presumably by train, but he confirms the "liberal terms" being given, because he was earning 30s a week there. His letter also shows that he was not the only man moving north then. He mentions Tom Michell, William Harris and Peter Collins as all preparing to set out. There must have been quite an exodus from the area.

The New World was the goal for others and advertisements were frequent and enticing for people needing employment, wanting adventure, or lured on by dreams of gold. "The Alchymist...is appointed to sail on the 25th of this month, for St. John's, New Brunswick. This very fast sailing vessel.....being fitted out on a superior scale for seaworthiness and comfort, is recommended to the choice of emigrants to British North America. Fare £3. Children and families at lower rates. Further information will be given by Foxes and Co., Perran Wharf, or by the master on board, at Restronguet." This appeared in the *West Briton* in 1832. With a ship so close how easy it might be for a local family to decide to go!

North America was the promised land for many. In 1841 George Trenhaile, an agricultural labourer, was living in Chycoose with his wife, Mary, and their three sons. In 1847 a George Trenhaile and his wife, Mary (nee Stephens), emigrated to Wisconsin. They are almost certainly the same family. The Stephens clan of Chycoose was numerous and some years later William Jenkin

Under Her Majesty's Commissioners.

ENTIRELY FREE
EMIGRATION
TO
VAN DIEMEN'S LAND
AND
New South Wales.

Mr. LATIMER,
OF TRURO,

Is desirous of obtaining, IMMEDIATELY, a LARGE NUMBER of Emigrants belonging to the class of *Mechanics*, Handicraftsmen, *Agricultural Laborers*, Carpenters, Quarrymen, Masons, and Domestic Ser ants.

The Emigrants must consist principally of married couples. Single women, with their relatives, are eligible, and in certain cases, *single men.*

The age of persons accepted as Adults is to be not less than 14, nor, generally speaking, more than 35 ; but the latter rule will be relaxed in favour of the parents of children of a working age.

The Colony of Van Diemen's Land has been established more than half-a-century, and possesses the usual advantages belonging to the Australian Settlements. It is not subject to drought, and affords a peculiar demand for the classes above-named.

No CHARGE for CHILDREN!!!

Applications, *post-paid*, or personal, to be made to Mr. LATIMER, 5 Parade, Truro.

E. HEARD. PRINTER AND BOOKBINDER. BOSCAWEN-STREET. TRURO.

Emigration Poster
Notice the encouragement given to families and skilled labour.
(Courtesy R.I.C.)

Stephens, son of the Devoran shipbuilder, Hugh Eddy Stephens, crossed the Atlantic for Brooklyn, New York. Another William who made the journey to America, was the elder son of Edward Bath of Trolver, who had left only a year or so before his parents were killed. (See section on Farming.)

In the early years of this century nearly all the brothers and sisters of one branch of the Michell family left for New Jersey. These were the four sons and two daughters of Thomas Michell, who was farming Trolver with his brother Ralph. They were mostly in their thirties, and had taken an active part in the life of the chapel, so their leaving must have created a vacuum difficult to fill.

It is noticeable that most of these came from a farming background and the timing of their emigration could be linked with periods when there were depressions in agriculture.

Australia on the far side of the world, with a long and dangerous voyage to endure, was the goal for others. A certain Samuel Stephens was "the first adult colonist to put foot on South Australian soil." He might well have been another Stephens of Chycoose as Samuel was a family name.

The Victorian gold rush of 1851 encouraged some to leave their native land for dreams of untold wealth. William Webber, a coal porter, left his wife and three sons behind in Point to try his luck in Australia. There were some men in this position who would then have made a new life for themselves with a new family, leaving the old one to struggle on as best it could. William's wife, Philippa, might well have wondered about her chances as she kept the family going by working as a charwoman. However this story seems to have a happy ending as William returned to her, and he ended his life in Point living on his own means as a retired gold miner.

Elizabeth Stephens married Stephen Brabyn, a bargeman from Point, in the Wesleyan Chapel in Truro in 1889. She had been born in Australia in about 1857, presumably because her parents had emigrated, but when or why she returned is not known.

Emigration was a possible solution for unemployment, dissatisfaction or just a way of getting rid of unwanted people. In 1860 the Feock Vestry Book records a recommendation "to give money not exceeding £10" to Bridget Clymo, to pay her passage, with her son, to Australia. Was this a generous gesture or an easy way to relieve the parish of a burden?

The years following the collapse of copper mining in Cornwall show a drop in the population of the area as well as an increase in the average age. In 1891 the numbers of people living around Point Green had fallen from about ninety to fifty-eight and although the number of households was much the same, many had only one or two older people living in them, unlike the bustling families of the past. There were also some homes where grandparents were looking after young children, perhaps because parents were trying to establish new homes elsewhere before their children joined them.   A number of these younger

71

people who moved away almost certainly emigrated.

Did all those who emigrated adapt to their new life successfully? Did they regret their decision to leave? Were their hopes fulfilled? Unfortunately this subject poses more questions than it answers.

To Sail the First of April,
1841,

FOR QUEBEC,

The fine fast sailing, British-built, Copper bolted BARQUE

VITTORIA,

650 Tons Burthen,

Mosey Simpson, Commander,

LYING AT MALPUS, IN TRURO RIVER,

Has very superior accommodation for Steerage and Cabin Passengers.

The Commander having been many years in the North American Trade, can give much valuable information regarding the Colonies, to any that may feel disposed to take a passage in the said ship.

Apply to the CAPTAIN on board,

Mrs. SIMPSON, at the Seven Stars Inn, Truro,

Or to the Owner, NICHOLAS MITCHELL, Malpus.

Dated, February 13th, 1841.

E. HEARD, PRINTER, BOOKBINDER, &c. BOSCAWEN-STREET, TRURO.

(Courtesy R.I.C.)

72

PART 2

PARTLY LEISURE

Donkey and trap
similar to one belonging to the Hitchens Family

The Mabel at Malpas Regatta in the late 1890s   *(Courtesy Mr. R. Bird)*

CHAPTER TEN

SMUGGLING

Work is only one aspect of everyday life; there are many other facets which would give a more complete picture of village life in the past. Much of this has not been recorded and can only be guessed at from little pieces of evidence and from childhood memories. One such piece of evidence shows angry Point people ready to defend their illicit dealings from the power of the law.

The eighteenth century was the golden age of smuggling. There was no income tax then, the only direct taxes being on land and windows, and most government money came from indirect taxation on goods from customs and excise duties. Imported wines and spirits, tea and coffee, tobacco and chocolate often attracted high rates. Brandy could be bought in France for 5s a gallon but cost 32s in England after duty had been paid. Gin was 2s a gallon in Holland but cost 8s in England. The incentives for smuggling were obviously high. Even during the Napoleonic Wars with France in the early nineteenth century, smuggling across the Channel continued, if on a reduced scale. When the Battle of Waterloo ended the wars in 1815 the incentive was still there and perhaps even greater as times were hard, bread expensive and wages low. The hard-pressed and under-resourced customs

Custom-House, London,

May 28, 1822.

WHEREAS it has been represented to the Commissioners of his Majesty's Customs, that Mr. JOHN TIPPETT, the Collector at the Port of *Truro,* did on the Morning of the 28th April last. make seizure of fifty-nine Kegs of Foreign Spirits, in a Barn or Out-house, at Point, in The Parish of *Feock,* in the County of *Cornwall,* and that about Five o'Clock in the Afternoon of the same Day: four of the said Kegs were rescued by Persons unknown, out of the custody of CHARLES PASCOE, who was left in charge of the said Kegs.

The said Commissioners, in order to bring to Justice the said Offenders, are hereby pleased to offer a Reward of

£20

to any Person or Persons. who shall discover or cause to be discovered any one or more of the Persons who rescued the said Kegs of Spirits. so that he or they may be apprehended and dealt with according to Law: to be paid by the Collector of His Majesty's Customs at the Port of *Truro.* upon Conviction.

By Order of the Commissioners.

G. DELAVAUD,

Reward notice in the *West Briton* after the smuggling episode in Point, 1822.

officers could not hope to overcome the problem, so smuggling was rife and a generally accepted activity by many people.

How much smuggling was carried on in this area is impossible to tell. Records are not often kept of illegal actions, so it is only when they have been

75

discovered and the processes of the law are put in motion, that we usually learn about them. There was certainly plenty of legal shipping activity to provide cover for the illicit trade.

The smuggling episode in 1822 had a curtain raiser a few months earlier. The revenue cutter, *Fox,* acting on information, had taken possession of a boat with Thomas Luke on board, although the officials seemed more anxious to catch Thomas Rogers. Both Luke and Rogers were local men and the story circulating in Point was that Charles Elliot of Loe, lieutenant of the Second Veteran Battalion, had sneaked on them telling the customs officials, "that Thomas Rogers had fitted out a boat and gone to Guernsey."

William Stevens, of Penpol Farm, had mentioned this rumour to Thomas Nicholas, a Truro solicitor and the story spread. There was an immediate denial from the Customs that Charles Elliott had told them anything about Luke or Rogers. The following week the *West Briton* published a letter from Stevens and Nicholas giving the details as they saw them and expressing surprise at this denial. Five months later customs officials found fifty-nine kegs of smuggled spirits in Thomas Rogers' barn at Point.

This barn was near the Bell Inn, which looked down over Point Green to Daniell's Quay. It is perhaps the barn still standing between Point House and the two nearest cottages, which were originally the inn. The customs officers had no suitable transport for these kegs, so they had to go off to St. Mawes for a boat, leaving one of the officers, Charles Pascoe, to guard them. This must have taken some time, whether they went by small boat or by horseback across the King Harry Ferry. There was certainly time for Point people to organise some resistance.

On the return of the customs officers they found that four of the kegs were missing. How this happened we can only guess. Presumably Charles Pascoe's attention had been distracted for a time while the kegs were sneaked out and hidden. The officers were determined to find them and began a search of the nearby fields and gardens.

Elizabeth Nicholls, the innkeeper's daughter, was busy sowing seeds when one of the officers began to prod the newly-turned soil. He found one jar containing three and a half gallons of brandy, and half an anker of gin. This was a cask that would hold about four gallons. He stopped Elizabeth from leaving the garden at gun point but was then accosted by a woman, probably Elizabeth's mother, brandishing a fire shovel. She tried to prevent him removing the containers and when this failed she attempted to break the jar, presumably to destroy evidence. She did not succeed but by this time a hostile crowd was gathering.

The man who acted as spokesman for the local people was Rogers, no doubt the same "ungentlemanly person" who had so annoyed John Swan at the opening of Lemon Quay four years earlier in 1818. (See section on Shipping.) He angrily denied the right of the customs men to search people's gardens threatening that "they would not escape with whole bones" if they had acted

76

like that in his garden. He argued that as he was the parish constable he had the authority there and not the officers.

Undeterrred, the customs officers loaded the barrels on to their boat, with the people pressing around them obviously in an ugly mood. As they hastily climbed on board, one of the officers was kicked in the back and a volley of stones was hurled after them. This they returned by firing their pistols over the heads of the crowd as the boat moved off.

Eleven months later Rogers was charged at Launceston Assizes "with having in concert with persons unknown obstructed and assaulted the officers of the customs in the execution of their duty." No one seems to have come forward with information to claim the £20 reward, which would have been a lot of money then. Rogers was found guilty of assault but not of obstruction. The newspaper account does not record his sentence.

Smuggling slowly decreased after this, partly because in that same year, 1822, the National Coast Guard was established to provide a more effective watch on the coasts. Also a change in government policy began the gradual reduction of customs duties, so making smuggling less profitable. Between 1822 and 1824 the authorities recovered 130,000 gallons of brandy and 227,900 gallons of gin and no doubt the Point haul is included in these statistics. Another obstacle to smuggled goods being brought ashore at Point was the appointment of a customs officer in the village.

Richard Chellew came from St. Ives with his wife and large family some time in the 1830s. He had been in the customs service for more than ten years so he was a well-established and experienced officer. He remained in Point until his death in 1862. As his house overlooked the road from the quay, the green and the front of the Bell Inn he was in an excellent position to keep an eye on the comings and goings in the village. The census of 1861 also records a tidewaiter, or at least his wife, whose job would have been to check the cargoes on board the boats in the creek. No more officials are recorded after this so perhaps Point was no longer considered important enough for its own officer. (See section on the Chellews.)

CHAPTER ELEVEN

MEETING PLACES

1) INNS

The Bell Inn
*The brick arch in the middle of the wall in these two cottages probably
shows the original doorway to the inn.*

There are no inns here now but in the nineteenth century there were three places to refresh the thirsty workers, although two of them were only short-lived. First and foremost there was the Bell Inn. This was probably established soon after Daniell's Quay was built and it looked down over the Green across Restronguet Creek. Its name is thought to have come from a bell kept outside for summoning a ferryman from Carnon Yard.

There was no restriction on opening times in these early days so drink would be available according to need and no doubt the whims of the innkeeper. The smuggling incident shows that duty-free spirits could be available to cheer the hearts of the pack horse drivers, lime burners, coal porters and bargemen after their hard, physical work. No doubt many a convivial hour was spent here.

Inns could also fulfil other functions for the community. Auction sales were sometimes held and meetings took place. The first record of the Bell was in 1817 when there was a notice of a survey to be held here for tenants of the area on Lord Falmouth's estates. Others are recorded in 1827, 1835 and 1858.

The Feock Vestry Book records parish meetings held here, especially in the 1840s. At these meetings decisions were made on the local poor rate, how much people owed and sometimes who would be exempted from paying. The state of the parish roads was discussed; for example the meeting of 1847 mentions the need to keep the road from Point to Tregoose in good repair. The important men of the parish would be unlikely to have their meetings in the public bar, so the inn was large enough to have private rooms.

Thomas Kempe and his wife had the licence for over thirty years; from some time before 1851 until the early 1880s. During this time and earlier, when Daniel Deeble was innkeeper in the 1830s and early 1840s, no dubious publicity affected the Bell, but in the 1880s when John Bridger had taken over the licence, it featured in the local paper on three separate occasions.

In January 1884 John Bridger was charged with selling adulterated gin. He said that he sold it to his customers for 2s a pint but if it was bought as it was sent to him it would cost 2s 3d. When a sample of his gin was tested it was found to be forty-two below proof. He was fined £5 with costs. The selling of gin by the pint perhaps indicates the popularity of these spirits once known as "mother's ruin."

Only three months later he was back in court again, this time for serving drinks after hours. To curb drunkenness Gladstone's government had passed a Licensing Act in 1872 to limit the hours when drink could be sold. It had been very unpopular with some people and Gladstone had attributed his failure in the general election of 1874 to this act. The magistrates in Truro were told how Police Constable Rickard, on duty in Point, visited the Bell at about 10.30 and found James Abbot drinking there. He was a mariner who lived with his family just below the Green, where his father-in-law, James Crago, had once kept a beershop. John Bridger could have been fined £10 for this but the magistrates were lenient, fining him only £1 with costs. James Abbot was fined 2s.6d plus costs. It is interesting to note that the fine for watering down the gin had been much higher than for drinking after hours.

Two years later Margaret Bridger, John's eighteen-year-old daughter, was in court to obtain an affiliation order against John Hearle Martin for the upkeep of her illegitimate child. Martin's solicitor referred to a meeting that had taken place earlier between Martin, the girl and her mother, implying that Martin had been drunk at the time, in spite of his being a member of the Band of Hope for some years. (Obviously a temperance society.) When the mother objected to this insinuation the solicitor suggested that she might have watered down his drink knowing of this membership. Was he perhaps trying to take advantage of John Bridger's previous record? These comments caused some amusement in the court, but the claim was upheld and Martin was ordered to pay two shillings and sixpence a week for fourteen years.

Within a few years the Bell closed down. No mention is made of an innkeeper in the census returns of 1891. No doubt with the mining activities finished and smelting and shipping on a greatly reduced scale the demand was less and perhaps the brewery did not find this a profitable concern any longer.

By this time there was no other inn in the immediate neighbourhood. The beershop that James Crago had once kept near the quay had been long closed. Unlike an inn, beershops, or kiddleywinks as they were often known, were only licensed to sell beer and not spirits, but it was not unknown for a drop to be available from under the counter. He was recorded in the 1841 census as a beershop keeper, but later he was described as a grocer.

Penpol had its own inn for a time near the bridge, no doubt much smaller than the Bell. Mathew Stevens (Stephens) had been a porter and then a lead smelter but in his old age, in the 1860s and 1870s, he became an innkeeper. His daughter Elizabeth and her husband Peter Pascoe, might not have been too happy over this, because many Methodists supported the temperance movement, but in the days before old age pensions and when wages were low, many old people needed to keep working for as long as possible. The threat of the workhouse could never have been far away.

Penpol was the site for the other important meeting place in the area - the Methodist Chapel.

Temperance Card showing that Charles Rees "took the pledge" when he was about twelve years old. He was exhorted to "Refrain under any pretence whatever from attending at the public-house" and to "remember that ale, beer, wine, spirits and other intoxicating liquors, are never necessary nor even useful to persons in health."

(Courtesy Mr. and Mrs. D. Rees)

2) PENPOLL WESLEYAN CHAPEL

The chapel at Penpol is tucked into the hillside overlooking the bridge, with trees above and a steep, grassy bank below covered with primroses and bluebells in the spring. On Thursday November 18th 1992, it celebrated the completion of a full-scale refurbishment with an open day and services. Chairs have replaced pews, concrete has replaced wood for the floor, new window frames have been installed, and walls have been replastered and repainted inside and out. This has all been achieved by contributions and the energy and enthusiasm of its members organising money-raising efforts from jumble sales and ploughman's lunches, to a barbecue, safari supper and a marathon sponsored walk of over 30 miles along the Saints' Way by two of the more intrepid members.

The same energy and enthusiasm were apparent over 130 years ago amongst a group of local people who had the faith and confidence, if not the money, to build this chapel. John Wesley had been dead for 70 years by then, so it is unlikely that any of them would have heard one of his rousing sermons which had such a profound effect on so many Cornish people. Grandparents might have heard him preach in Boscawen Street in Truro or great-grandparents could have been part of "a very large congregation," as Wesley described his listeners at Perranwell in 1747. But if they had not heard him they might well have been one of the hundreds at Gwennap Pit, which continued to draw in crowds every Whit Monday.

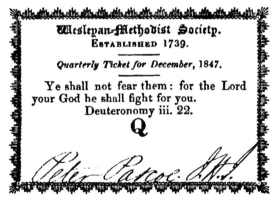

Wesleyan-Methodist Society.
Established 1739.

Quarterly Ticket for December, 1847.

Ye shall not fear them: for the Lord your God he shall fight for you.
Deuteronomy iii. 22.

Q

A Methodist Society was formed in Penpol some time after 1841 as part of the Perranwell Circuit, perhaps in 1847 when Peter Pascoe and his wife Elizabeth were given class tickets, and then five years later it was transferred to the Gwennap Circuit. Little is known of the chapel which these early worshippers used, but it must have become inadequate for its purpose because plans were soon made for the larger building which is there now.

Richard Harris, the carpenter who lived higher up the valley, played a crucial role in these plans. He was granted a 99 year lease in 1856 by the Trelissick estate for the land and building "lately used as a Meeting House or Chapel." The lease was subject to the usual three lives, himself, his 25-year-old daughter Catherine and his 19-year-old son Edwin. Six years later, when the new chapel was built, he assigned the premises to nine Trustees. These were himself, Edwin now married and living with his wife and baby son at Come-to-Good, Thomas White the schoolteacher at the Feock Lead Smelting

School, William Williams of Penpol Farm, William Maunder a leadsmelter living in Chycoose and later to keep a shop on Point Green, two other smelters John Treneale and Robert Sampson, Thomas Martin a sawyer who lived on Point Green with his large family, and William Plummer a millwright.

On Good Friday 1861 a public tea was held to begin the task of raising the necessary money. Many local people contributed but the overall amount was small compared with the costs. William Williams gave ten shillings and the milk for the tea, William Chellew and his wife also contributed ten shillings, but most offerings were five shillings or less. Subscriptions the following year brought in over £40, but money had to be borrowed, £150 in 1861 and £120 the following year, when the bills began to roll in.

Gunpowder was bought for blasting out a larger site; 875 bricks cost £1.7s; Delabole slate was transported to Falmouth by sea and then carted for 3s.6d to Penpol; granite cost £8.9s. Richard Harris must have done the bulk of the work himself because he was paid £200 for materials and labour, but many others played their part. William Mellen the miller received 1s.6d for the use of his horse and cart, Thomas Pearce was paid for a number of jobs including 9s. for bringing the slates from Falmouth and with John Gay 10s.6d for fetching bricks.

Penpoll Chapel

As the main structure was finished so the furnishings were purchased. A carpet and mat cost 11s.3d, lights for the pulpit £2.10s and a chandelier was bought for the princely sum of £8.5s.4d. These accounts were meticulously recorded by Thomas White as Treasurer and he did not forget the important detail of 7s.7d for brushes, dust pan and a floor cloth.

All these people must have felt some pride and happiness when the opening service was finally held on 30th January 1862. The day was a very full one with a morning service followed by dinner, then a bazaar in the afternoon, by which time the tea provided must have been welcome. The occasion was rounded off by an evening meeting. Some people there might have had niggling worries over the cost, because the debt was not finally paid off until 1908.

The parish church at Feock still continued to be used by some, but it must have seemed a long way to walk, especially on a wet day, when there was a place of worship on the doorstep. It was certainly still used as the setting for weddings: John Gay was married there in 1863, William William's daughters, Emma and Ellen, both had their weddings there, as did Thomas Martin's two daughters in 1866 and 1871. Those who wanted a Methodist service had to go to the Wesleyan Chapel in Truro: Elizabeth Stephens married Stephen Brabyn there in 1889, and four years later William Chellew's daughter Bessie held her wedding there. It was not until much later that marriages were licensed in Penpol and Graham Crocker's parents were the first to take advantage of this in 1927.

The new chapel must have strengthened the community, not only by providing a convenient place of worship, but also by becoming a focus for the area in other ways. A Sunday School had already been established connected with the day school, and before long a small single-storey schoolroom was built on to the end of the chapel and the Sunday school transferred there. (See following section.) This school room and the chapel were in demand by other people and organisations, especially when the closure of the Bell Inn made these the only community rooms in the area, until the opening of the Mission Room on Point Green.

Parish Council meetings were held here including the first one under the Local Government Act of 1894. Much of this meeting and the one held the following year, again in the schoolroom, was concerned with an obstruction on Point Green caused by William Chellew, the timber merchant, when strong feelings were expressed, especially on the second occasion. In 1897 the main question was whether the water supply in Point was adequate. It was suggested that the sinking of a new well might make other places in the parish feel neglected and no decision was made.

The chapel and schoolroom have continued to be used for community affairs throughout this century. The committee of the new St. Feock Garden Society held meetings there after the First World War, and in more recent years it has been the venue for the Penpol and Point Women's Institute, surprisingly one of the largest branches in the county.   The original schoolroom would have been uncomfotably crowded for this, but in 1961 a larger building replaced it. Neighbourhood Watch meetings have been held in the chapel, a sign of community concern, which was also shown on another recent occasion when local people came close to losing access to Point Quay. This would have heralded disaster for the famous annual regatta.

The Penpoll Chapel Choir in the early years of this century
Back: William Rees, William Michell, George Reed, Harry Rees, Martin Cock, Sam Mennear
Middle: Lena Crocker, Annie Trenhaile, Mary Annie Marshall, Flora Michell, Flora May Marshall, Sam Lilly
Front: Charlie Rees, Laura Cock, ?, Edith Rees (wife of Harry), Miss Mole, Violet Wasley.
(Courtesy Mrs. H. Michell)

Music has been a constant source of enjoyment whether as part of a service or just as an entertainment. Moody and Sankey Hymn Books were used for the chapel which had a choir, and for the school; in 1877 three dozen were bought for the school anniversary. Ten years later a resolution was made by the Sunday School teachers "to ask Miss Chellew to get up a service of song" for the afternoon Anniversary Service. A band was an important part of the annual Tea Treat for the Sunday School, helping to make it a day to remember but during the First World War, when it was not available, it was decided to have singing instead during the march around the pond.

84

An amusing story is told about one concert held in the chapel on the evening of Easter Monday some time in the 1890s. Young Marjory Trethowan, picked to sing in a duet, was caught on the mud in her rowing boat by the ebbing tide earlier in the day. She was not made any happier by spectators laughing at her from the beach, or by her brothers' efforts to "help" when they threw apples at her. As she furiously flung them back she partly over-balanced, getting splattered with mud before the incoming tide finally rescued her from her ordeal. The emotions of the day proved too much; in her moment of glory at the chapel that evening her duet contribution was off-beat and out-of-tune.

Many concerts must have taken place which have left no record, but there are glimpses of some occasions, even if we do not know what songs were sung. In 1909 Mrs. Woolcock, formerly Bessie Chellew, was granted the use of the schoolroom for an entertainment "providing that the return concert be given in aid of the Sunday School." The following year she was asked to "get up a concert " for the school. In 1916, during the First World War, a concert was organised in aid of soldiers and sailors. The posters for 1932 show more money-raising efforts and a concert for the converting of the chapel from oil lighting to electricity.

All these activities based on the chapel brought together smelter and captain, farmer amd farm worker, tradesman and mariner, men and women, young and old, in a way that possibly no other organisation could have done. Although membership has dropped, with fewer children amongst a growing number of retired people, the chapel still brings people together, especially the newcomers and the older-established families.

Oil lamps in the Chapel before electricity was installed
(Courtesy Mr. and Mrs. G. Crocker)

PENPOLL WESLEYAN CHAPEL.

NEW

ELECTRIC LIGHTING SCHEME.

AND DECORATION SCHEME,

LATER ON.

THE OPENING

of the former will take place on

Friday, Jan. 15th, 1932.

Preaching Service at 3.45, by Rev. J. F. EATON.

Public Tea at 5 p.m.   Prices 9d. & 6d.

-: PUBLIC MEETING at 7 p.m., :-

when Mr. W. H. CORNEW, of Truro, will take the Chair,
supported by the Revs. J. F. Eaton and G. Riley Mallinson, with

Mrs. HOWARD HEARLE, of Devas, Ponsanooth,

who will perform the Opening Ceremony of the new lights.

After the Meeting there will be a COFFEE SUPPER.

ALL COLLECTIONS IN AID OF NEW LIGHTING AND DECORATION SCHEME.

W. REES, Sec. to the Trust,
Penpoll, Devoran, Truro.

J. A. CLEAVE, Printer, Stationer, Bookseller, Etc., 14, PYDAR STREET, TRURO.

Lighting Up Time at Penpoll Chapel
(Courtesy Mr. and Mrs.D. Rees)

PENPOL WESLEYAN CHAPEL.

SALE OF WORK

for Electric Light Installation & Re-decoration,

will take place in the SCHOOLROOM, on

Friday, March 11th, 1932.

THE OPENING CEREMONY

will be performed at 3 p.m., by

MRS. B. B. CHELLEW WOOLCOCK, (POINT),

supported by

Rev. G. RILEY MALLINSON.

There will be

STALLS of Useful and Fancy Articles, Sweets, Fruit,
Vegetables, Flowers, &c., & other attractions.

REFRESHMENTS AT NOMINAL CHARGES.

From 7.15 p.m. to 8.15 p.m.

A CONCERT

will be given in the CHAPEL, by

CARNON DOWNS GLEE SINGERS.

A COLLECTION WILL BE TAKEN FOR THE ABOVE FUND.

W. REES, Sec. to the Trust.

J. A. CLEAVE, Printer, Stationer, Bookseller, Etc., 14, PYDAR STREET, TRURO.

Mrs. Chellew Woolcock doing the Honours
(Courtesy Mr. and Mrs.D. Rees)

Zone 23 January 1854

My little darling Fanny

I received your little note and I am delighted to see that you are getting on so well with your writing and ciphering and I hope you will continue to improve and be a good girl and if I live to see you I will reward you for it Give my kind love to your Mistress and to Mr White and to Grandfather & Grandmother and all your Uncles and aunts and your little Cousins and your little school mates and I hope after a little while to have a long letter from you telling me all the news you know, give my kind love to your Brothers & Sisters and kiss them for me, and I will pay you again, so no

More at present from your affectionate Father

P Pascoe

good bye my little

darling

Fanny Pascoe would have been eight years old when she received this letter from her father, who was obviously doing his best to encourage her in her reading and writing. Thomas White and Jane Hocking, Fanny's "Mistress," were the teachers then at the local school, established by Robert Michell for the children of the lead workers.

Before schools were started many children would have been expected to work, often with their parents, from quite a young age, such as twelve-year-old Nicholas May working as a shoemaker with his father at Point in 1841. Families were frequently large, which could bring both companionship and responsibilities. Girls would be expected to look after younger members of the family and sometimes had full responsibility for a household in their mid-teens. In 1851 the household of widower, John Nettle, son of the lead works manager, James Nettle, consisted of five sons from the age of four to sixteen and two daughters. The elder one, fourteen-year-old Emma, was housekeeper helped by her twelve-year-old sister, Mary. At least the younger children were away from home during some of the day as they are all described as "scholars" in the census.

The Feock Lead Works School

Exactly when the Feock Lead Works School began is not clear. A schoolmistress, Elizabeth Thomas, is recorded living in Penpol in 1841 but she might have had just a dame school. The first definite mention seems to be in the following extract from the *West Briton* of July 1848 when Mr. Davies Gilbert of Trelissick gave a tea treat to all the schools in Feock parish. "About two o'clock in the afternoon, the steamer Sydney was seen crossing the river towards Trelissick, and soon discharged the children and their friends. From Point the scholars of the school established by Mr. Michell, and conducted on the British and Foreign system, were conveyed in waggons, with appropriate banners, whilst the children belonging to the other schools in the parish were seen walking in procession. At length the whole assembled in front of the mansion, where every preparation was made for their reception."

So at least twenty-two years before Forster's Act of 1870 made education a possibility for all children, Point/Penpol already had its own school and this would have been the main meeting place for many of the children.

The 1861 census records that the school was at Rope House but little more is known about it. It was run, as the West Briton shows, on the British and Foreign system, which was organised by the Nonconformists, unlike the National School in Feock itself, which was an Anglican foundation. Both types of school used the monitorial system. This meant that the teacher taught a small group of older children who then passed on their knowledge parrot-fashion to the younger children. This method was not designed for original thinking, an unnecessary accomplishment, but was satisfactory for the learning of limited knowledge which could then be easily tested. Maybe the present government would approve of this system. But whatever its limitations it was no doubt better than no education at all. The ability to read could open up new worlds.

Equipment would have been very basic, with writing being practised on slates. In 1867 the Wesleyan Sunday School, which shared the same premises for a time, gave £1 to the day school for books and slates.

Children at Point Green in the early years of this century. (Courtesy RIC)

Thomas White was the schoolmaster for at least twelve years, but he left in the 1860s and in 1871 Priscilla Jenkin, a woman in her early twenties, was the schoolmistress. There might have been a bit of nepotism here because her father was an assayer, but whether in the lead works or the newly-begun tinworks is not clear.

In 1880 when the lease was drawn up for the Penpoll Tin Smelting Works the exceptions included, "a certain plot of the said premises sometime since granted to the said Robert Michell for the purpose of building a School Room." No teacher is recorded in the census returns from 1881 but Kelly's Directory describes Georgina Rees as a schoolmistress. However the census records her as a milliner, so perhaps she conducted a dame school in her home in Penpol while making her hats, after the closure of the Lead Smelting School.

Private School

When the day school closed at Point many children had to go to school in Feock or Devoran. For some this meant the village schools; for others it could be one of the small private schools that were prevalent before the First World War. Devoran had several of these and a glimpse of Miss Farquharson's School is given by Joyce Ritchie, niece of Marjory Trethowan, who had such an unfortunate experience at a concert in Penpoll Chapel. (See previous section.) Marjory and some of her brothers and sisters went to this school for a time.

She was of the "old school" - a fine teacher and a great disciplinarian. Any child who was not taught to behave properly at home was soon aware that rigid self-control was the first and foremost necessity, if he were to escape the quiet scorn of her tongue and be made the centre of attention in an unfortunate manner. They had to sit up perfectly erect; any child who found this too much of a bore was provided with a "backboard", a stiff plank-like contraption, which was strapped to their backs until they felt capable of sitting upright unaided. This was usually fairly soon, because although the board was not as uncomfortable as it sounds, the wearing of it was not considered exactly "mature". They were discouraged from hanging their heads and if guilty, they were issued with stiff cardboard collars to wear. Only a few days at the most of these aids were required and the carriage and the angle at which the head was held, distinguished many of the pupils of Miss Farquharson for the rest of their lives. The Dunce sat on the end, or bottom seat of the class, and the top girl was rewarded by wearing a most beautiful bracelet whilst she retained top marks, and the top boy wore a gold watch. By these simple but psychologically clever manoeuvres did this old and astute scholar mould the character, as well as the minds, of more than one generation of children.

Penpoll Wesleyan Sunday School

Thomas White, besides being the schoolmaster, had also been a Trustee and Treasurer for the Wesleyan Chapel during its first few years and a close connection existed between the day school and the chapel. The Sunday School was held in the rooms of the Lead Works School until the chapel built its own schoolroom in 1869. This could cause problems as the Sunday School Journal for December 1863 records. "In consequence of the Master of the Boys' Day School having kept the keys of the cupboard the teachers could not get at the Books - a prayer meeting was held." It was probably a shorter session than usual on that occasion. When the new chapel schoolroom was built the pupils of the day school contributed 5s 7d towards it.

The school involved a large number of children and adults. In 1868, about eighteen months before the move to the new schoolroom, the numbers were high: 143 children and 55 teachers. They must have been cramped in their new premises, so the decision recorded in the Teachers' Minutes for 1881 is not surprising, except for the fact that it did not come sooner: "the Adult class be put into the Chapel for the convenience of the school." Instruction consisted of learning the Catechism, spelling, hymn singing and questions on the Scriptures, according to the minutes for 1880.

A system of rewards was used to encourage regular attendance, as this entry shows, made soon after the move into the new premises. "It was resolved that the scale of Rewarding of the children be the same as that adopted in the old school with the exception of the Bible classes. They to be rewarded as follows. Those that have been absent 4 times in the year 1s, 8 times 8d., 12 times 4d. The children to be rewarded by the officers of the school the first Sunday in the New Year if possible."

One reason for absence could be the weather. An entry in the attendance book for 1862 states: "A very wet afternoon which accounts for the very small attendance." Only 34 children were there with 12 teachers, and similar comments were made on later occasions.

By 1900 the numbers were falling, reflecting the changes in the population. The average age of the people was rising as job opportunities fell, so there were fewer children, only 74 registered with 37 in the two adult classes. Thirty years later these had fallen further and this trend has continued as the younger people have moved away, so that in recent years the Sunday School has had to close.

Certain families have played a large part in the school both as pupils and as teachers. In a quick flip through the pages of the attendance registers the name Michell is very prominent, with many members of this family, some of them farmers at Trolver, appearing again and again. It must have been a big blow to the school and the chapel when almost all the brothers and sisters of one of the branches of the family emigrated to the U.S.A in the early years of this century, but others remained. Rees, Crocker, Hitchens and Chegwyn are also names that recur; all are recorded in the 1890s and are still there in the 1950s. Some are familiar in the neighbourhood today.

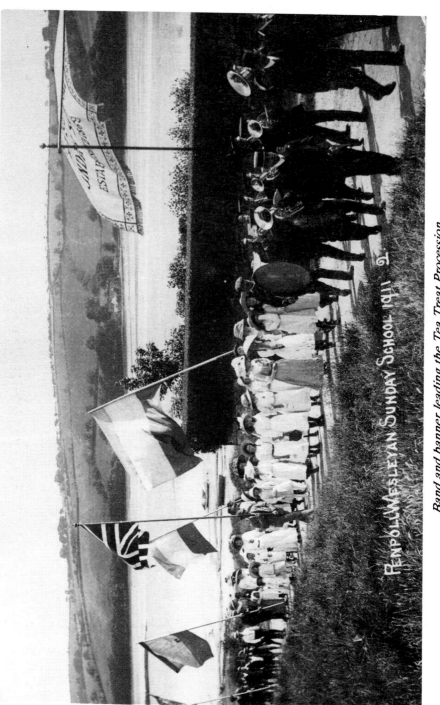

PENPOL WESLEYAN SUNDAY SCHOOL 1911

Band and banner leading the Tea Treat Procession
"Junket Cottage" in the background   (Courtesy Mr and Mrs. R. Michell)

4) THE MISSION ROOM

For a time a mission hall was opened in one of the cottages on the Green. This was connected with the new parish of Devoran, created in 1873, which had taken over Feock's land west of the Penpol Valley. Afternoon services were held there with Mrs. Chellew Woolcock accompanying the singing. When it was used for concerts during the First World War to raise money for the troops, people filled the little room and overflowed up the stairs.

5) JACK'S HOUSE

In the earlier years of this century there were two places where the old men would meet for a smoke and a gossip. On fine days they sat by the old lime kiln (Jack's House), where wooden benches placed by the arch would catch the morning sun. If it was cold or wet they went to the reading room. This was a single-room building beside the cottages leading up to the Green. (See colour section - the painting by Charles Rees.) There they could play dominoes in comfort by the fire, unless one of the mischievous boys climbed up to the top of the chimney to block it and send smoke billowing out into the room, which was not unknown.

Tea Treat Group: Charles Rees in bowler hat on the right. Hazel Searle
(Mrs. Michell) with her sister Doris wearing brimmed hats near centre front.
(Courtesy Mrs. H. Michell)

93

CHAPTER TWELVE

TEA TREATS, BOATS
AND MORE

"Hot, sweet tea from an enamel jug .....
tea never tasted as well again."

A summer's afternoon, the beat of a band, the chatter of excited children, the march behind the blue and gold banner clutching mugs in warm hands, the smiles and waves, the wide hats of the ladies at the tea table, the huge, yellow saffron buns, the games, the singing - all these made up the Sunday School Anniversary Tea Treat.

Every year the Sunday School teachers organised fund raising, ordered the food, booked a band and arranged the venue. The first record is in the Teachers' Minute Book for 1866 when collectors were appointed to raise money, not just in the immediate neighbourhood, but as far as Mylor and Perran Foundry. Peter Pascoe collected £4 8s from the lead works towards the overall total of £14 15s 11d.

The provisions seemed to be carefully shared out between local people, especially in the earlier years. In 1869 for instance:

Mr. Bath (Trolver) for Milk and Butter	2s 2d
Mr. Michell (Trolver) for Milk and Butter	1s 0d
Mr. Daniell (Chycoose) for Milk and Butter	3s 1d
Mr. Williams (Penpol) for Milk and Butter	1s 3d

Music was an important part of the occasion. In 1873 the Minute Book records that Charles George was to be invited "to get a few friends to play music." But one well-remembered group was the Hungarian Band, first mentioned in 1899 and invited back regularly for some years.

A field was obtained for the big day: in 1883 a field at Penpol "kindly lent by Mr. Williams." The following year it was held "up in Mr. Daniell's Moor." In 1885 "in one of Mr. Chellew's meadows at Point if we can have permission." Eight years later they decided to ask "Mr. Teague (manager of the tinworks) if one of his meadows could be used." But for many years it was held in one of Mr. Michell's fields at Trolver, where the houses of Trevallion Park are now built.

These occasions seem filled with happy childhood memories, as the quotation from Mrs. Nancy Hibbert at the beginning shows. She also remembers the pansy buttonholes carefully made every year and given to each child by the Miss Hares, who lived beside the chapel.

*The Hall Family enjoying their Annual Picnic at Loe Beach.
Louisa Hall handing out the tea. (See page 23.)*

At Bone Mill, Penpol, in 1937. Richard Hitchens nearest to the camera.

REGATTAS
"The annual regatta, when all animosities are sunk and all of us
for one day at least are on best behaviour."
This quotation from Violet Whish's novel, *Come Four Winds*, sums up regatta
days as she knew them in the middle years of this century, when a barge could
arrive looking "as though it had survived the Spanish Armada."

Boats must always have played an important part in the life of the people
living around the creek both for work and leisure, but organised sailing races
became a feature of many seaside towns and villages during the nineteenth
century. Even before 1893 there was at least one regatta held here, as the
West Briton for July 19th 1870 shows. "An interesting regatta took place on
Thursday in Restronguet Creek, the general interest in the affair being
enhanced by the fact that the prizes were contributed by the mass of the
villagers." It was held from "the quay attached to the large smelting works
carried on by Messrs. Robert Michell and Sons."

This report gives details of two of the races, first for 16 foot and then for 14
foot boats, which "proved a very pretty one, the little craft going through the
water under an extraordinary pressure of canvas at great speed". This race
was won convincingly by William Harris of Trolver in his boat of that name.
Particular mention was made of "some yachts belonging to gentlemen in the
vicinity of Point," which included Humphrey Broad Champion's "splendidly
lined dandy." (See section on the Lead Smelting Works.)

As I am writing this (March 1993) plans are being made for the centenary
celebrations, for a band, an open-air service, a display of local crafts, a
twinning ceremony with the Breton village of L'Hôpital-Camfrout and a full
turn-out of working boats, in addition to the usual splendid teas provided for
visitors and crews.

Exciting though this may be it is less extrovert than the entertainments that
accompanied the regattas between the wars and in the years immediately
following. Then the Cornish sheaf-pitching championships were fought out,
greasy poles were climbed, or not as the case might be, feathers flew while
people, balancing on a narrow pole, bashed each other with pillows. Stalls, or
stennens, were set up lit by kerosene lamps, which sold sweets "better tasting
than in the shops," as Iris Dunstan recalls. A carnival parade was held when
ingenuity was tested to the full. Motor vehicles were adorned, and bicycles
decorated: Hazel Searle (Mrs. Michell) won first prize for her cycle in 1922,
Marion Chegwyn won the fancy dress costume as "Our Allotment," Harry
Crocker and Dan Hitchens gained the prize for humour as "Uncle Joe and
Aunt Sally," and Reg Crocker's "Onion Boy" won him a children's prize. The
day was finally rounded off by dancing on the lawn of Penpol House to the
music of the band of the training ship, *Foudroyant.*

In all this activity the boats seem forgotten but there were more than ten
sailing and rowing races for men and women, with the names of Ferris,
Hitchens, Crocker, Michell, Trebilcock and Bryant cropping up frequently in
the lists of winners.   Two familiar boats were *Flip Flap* and   *Grannie and*

PRETTY RIVER FESTIVAL

PENPOL AND POINT REGATTA AND CARNIVAL

Brilliant summer sunshine and a moderate North wind greatly enhanced the success of Penpol and Point regatta, held on Saturday. Large numbers of spectators gathered on the shore of the picturesque little creek, and even more assembled for the land sports and carnival in the evening. The entries were comparatively good, particularly in the sailing classes, in which competition was keen. There were 14 events, among which the race for the gigs of the Foudroyant, Falmouth, manned by the crew of the training ship, and gig and punt chase, in which these boats also participated, were especially fine. In the former race, "Yellow" obtained an easy first, but there was a close fight for second place between the "White" and "Red" boats, the "White" eventually winning. "Blue" secured fourth place. The gig and punt chase was particularly amusing.

Mr. L. D'Oliveyra was the president and chairman of the committee, Mr. G. H. May was treasurer and Mr. E. Trenoweth secretary. Mr. W. Crocker acted as starter.

West Briton, 1922

Grandpa, first and third in the working dredging boats race. (See Shipbuilding section.) Most of the boats were working boats of some sort; not an Optimist, Firefly or catamaran in sight in those days.

During the Second World War two successive regattas were held to raise money for the Red Cross, with the usual carnival procession. A water carnival was held in coronation year when, in the evening, specially decorated and lit boats sailed past the quay. That was the famous occasion when the Cunard liner *Queen Mary* sailed in the creek. If you do not believe this look at the photograph on page 98.

ROWING RACES

These were a regular feature on summer evenings, not just at regatta time. Most races were held in Devoran Creek, between Chycoose and Devoran, using skiffs and oyster dredging punts powered by the strong arms of a Trebilcock, Ferris or Bryant. Some of these boats were specially built for their speed by Tom Hitchens at Carnon Yard and Fred Bryant at Carnon Mine.

JUNKETINGS

A more leisurely enjoyment was to sail or row to Junket Cottage, as it was known. This was a thatched cottage, later burnt down, across Restronguet Creek near Halwyn, where junkets were the speciality. These were very popular desserts, as shown by the frequent advertisements of the time for rennet, which was used to make them. They certainly provided a good excuse for an afternoon jaunt. (See photo of the Tea Treat Procession - the cottage is in the distance down by the water.)

SHOOTING

The prevalence of guns today gives some people cause for concern. What seems surprising is the number owned by people in the past for leisure activity, or to provide food for the pot. Charles Rees, a young mason in his twenties, left the area with his bride in 1871 in response to the demand for coal miners in Scotland. Soon after he arrived he wrote to his sister, Sarah, and her

97

husband, Peter Pascoe, mentioning that he had promised to sell his gun to a friend for 6s. and that this money could be sent up to him when another friend joined him there.

A story is told of Ned Bath's "wickedly high spirits," when he and his nephew Fred Burley went out for a bit of shooting one day. They set off from Point, where Ned had a shop on the Green, and when they turned on to the Tram Road Ned raised his gun and "let off a blast the length of the empty lane." How would an action like this be regarded today? Luckily there was no harm done, but for another Point man his shooting expedition resulted in death.

The story is told in the *West Briton* in September 1887. "On Tuesday James Webber of Point with his brother and a young man named Marshall, went in a boat to St. Just for the purpose of shooting rabbits. Consequent on the grounding of the boat, when they were about to land, a gun, which was laid across two of the seats, slipped and went off. The charge grazed the arm of Marshall and struck Webber.....in his left side, passing right through him." It goes on to say how the other two rowed to the training ship Ganges for help but James was already dead.

CHILD'S PLAY

This section started with the excitement of the Sunday School tea treats and ends with childhood memories from the years between the wars: of swimming on Stamps Beach before Penpol Boatyard was built, of fetching the milk from Penpol Farm and swinging the can round without spilling a drop, of playing in "Golden Castle," the gorse-covered field above the Penpol Valley and of the joy of listening to the wireless. Mr. Whish supplied accumulators, which he charged at 6d a time and as Mrs. Nancy Hibbert says, "many a dark night we went to get another as it had just run out in the middle of a serial."

*Reg Crocker with his "Queen Mary" dressed overall in Coronation Year
(Courtesy Mr. R. Crocker)*

CHAPTER THIRTEEN

A WOMAN'S WORK ....

"The women are mostly dirty...there sleeves is turned up and no shoes nor stockings Sundays. The young women go out with there men to walk like that." So wrote Charles Rees about the Scottish women, when he moved to Ayrshire in 1871. The implication for the women he knew in Point and Penpol is clear.

It is difficult to gauge the influence that women had in the community, because much of their work was in the home, either theirs or someone else's, for which there is little information. When they married they not only changed their name, but might also move from their home area, so it is not easy to keep track of any individual. But one thing is certain: most women who did paid work were either unmarried or widowed.

NEEDLES AND SCOURERS
Look at the splendid hats of the ladies in the chapel choir or at the tea treat. (See pages 84 and 93.) These might well have been made locally because for much of the nineteenth century there was at least one milliner working in the area. In 1851 there were two "straw bonnet makers," Jane Bersey, sister of Samuel who began market gardening, and Thomasin Stevens, daughter of Mathew who later had the inn at Penpol. But the milliner with most years' experience was Georgina Rees, a sister of Charles Rees, who made hats for the women of Point and Penpol for at least thirty years.

The same two photographs show something of the tucks and frills of the women's blouses, quite possibly painstakingly home-made or done by a local dressmaker. During the second half of the last century there were several women who made money in this way. Georgina's eldest sister, Sarah, was a dressmaker before her marriage to Peter Pascoe and continued for some time afterwards, passing on her skills to her daughter, Annie. On Point Green there were four dressmakers in 1871 all in one household. These were the daughters of Thomas Martyn, sawyer, and his wife, Susan, who had one of the larger households in the area. How the sisters, ranging from fifteen to twenty-four, all managed to cut out and sew material in the small cottage rooms is difficult to imagine, especially if the light was not very good.

The larger farms and the middle-class families usually had servants, often living-in. In 1851 James Nettle, manager at the lead works, and his wife employed two housemaids, even though they only had one son living at home. Ten years later William Chellew, timber merchant, and his wife Elizabeth had four children all under seven. They employed a child's maid, a house servant and a young man as a general servant. Few women stayed in the same household for very long, but one exception was Emma Clinch, who was with the Chellew family when she was in her mid-twenties and still with them twenty years later.

Widowers, such as John Dunstan, sometimes employed a housekeeper. In 1851 he was a coal yard porter in his sixties with a blind son, Nicholas, who was a musician; elderly Jane Harris looked after this household. Often in these circumstances a daughter would take over the household duties as did fourteen-year-old Emma Nettle. (See section on Schools.) Emma's father, John, soon remarried, as did Peter Pascoe some years later when he was left a widower with young children to care for.

In many cases women would help in the family business, even if they were not officially regarded as employed. This was obviously true for farmers' wives and their daughters, and in some cases they continued running the concern after the death of their husband or father, as Elizabeth Williams did for a time at Penpol Farm after her father, William, died. When Thomas Kempe, innkeeper of the Bell, died his wife Mary continued to run it for over fifteen years.

FAMILY LIFE AND DEATH

Most women's lives were based on their house, husband and children. When the teenage bride and groom, Elizabeth Stevens and Peter Pascoe were married in 1843 they set up home with furniture made by the local carpenter, Richard Harris. A mahogany table cost £2 10s, a four post bedstead £2 12s, six birch chairs and "2 Elbows polished" came to £3 7s, a kitchen table, dressing table and stand were £1 13s and a wash tray cost 5s. In addition there was a maple table for 16s, the total coming to £11 3s 6d. Not exactly lavish, but no doubt considered adequate.

Many of the cottages were small: one or two rooms downstairs and the same above. Today these same cottages, modernised and enlarged, are considered ideal homes for a couple or a single person. In the last century they might have housed eight, ten or even more. The birth rate was high and families could be large. In 1861 Elizabeth and Peter Pascoe were living in one of the Rope House tenements with their nine children. In the following four years they had three more. Joanna and William Ferris, the shipbuilder, had eleven children. Julianna and Hugh Stephens, carpenter, probably had ten children in their Chycoose home. This overcrowding and lack of privacy would be unacceptable to many people today. In the case of Elizabeth and Richard Chellew, customs officer, the problem was solved by using two houses. In 1841 they lived on Point Green with five children and two servants while their two eldest sons, Richard and Francis, had some measure of independence next door. Most people would not have been able to afford this option.

Why were families so large? Birth control methods were of course very basic and not generally acceptable. An improvement in health, because the farming changes had made more fresh dairy produce and meat available, might have been another factor. Also large families could be an insurance for old age: with no state retirement pensions, many elderly people, even if they kept working for as long as possible, might end up dependent on their children or else it could be the dreaded workhouse. Whatever the reasons, there was a population explosion in the country as a whole. Between 1801 and 1851 the population of England (including Cornwall) and Wales almost doubled and it more than doubled itself between 1851 and 1911.

100

Mr. Hitchens coming to fetch water from the well at Penpol
(Courtesy Mr. and Mrs. I. Dunstan)

Mothers giving birth every year or so would need help. Relations were usually not far away, but children would be expected to play their part, looking after younger brothers and sisters as well as doing many small chores. One necessary job was fetching drinking water in earthenware pitchers. All houses would have a rain water butt for household tasks like doing the laundry, but drinking water had to come from the wells. Mains water only came to Point and Penpol in the 1950s, so there are many people who can remember fetching the water. (The Carnon Mine cottages were only put on the mains within the last few years.) The pump on Point Green was not set up until the 1930s and Mrs. Joyce Rees (Brabyn) can remember walking from Point to Chycoose with her grandfather to fetch water from the well there. Mrs. Iris Dunstan has a very clear memory of the sweet-tasting water from the well at Penpol, situated beside the stream below the farm. The tin smelters would also fill a barrel from the Penpol well every day.

Many parents had to suffer the deaths of their children, for if the birth rate was high, so was the death rate. The young children were especially vulnerable and it must have been heart-breaking for mothers, after bearing and caring for their babies, to see them die. Perhaps the overcrowding and the air pollution from the smelting works and lime kiln contributed towards the high mortality.

The summer of 1851 seems to have been a particularly bad time. While the Crystal Palace was filled with visitors for the Great Exhibition in Hyde Park marvelling at the variety of products on show, including some from this area, children were dying especially in Chycoose. Five members of the Stephens family, mostly under four years old, died in August and September, as well as three children from Point. Six years later there was another bad time when seven died, including another Stephens child, and also four-year-old William Chellew. The vicar rather than the curate officiated at his funeral. Does this show some class distinction? The parish register does not record any reason for this spate of deaths, but there were bad epidemics in the nineteenth century.

One feared killer was smallpox, and in 1871 this was recorded as the cause of death for young Hannah Harris of Trolver. This disease could be prevented by vaccination since Edward Jenner's experiments in the late eighteenth century, and this had become compulsory, with penalties for those who avoided it. Perhaps her parents had particular cause for regret.

The Stephens clan seemed especially prone to child mortality: in 1863 they had another tragedy, when seven-year-old Charles Stephens, nephew of the Carnon Yard shipbuilder, was drowned. The *West Briton* reported how his body had been found floating in the river near Point, "as he was a little boy fond of playing with boats it was supposed that he was amusing himself near the quay when he accidentally fell in the water." He seems to have inherited his mariner father's love of ships.

WIDOWS

There might well have been some merry widows in Point or Penpol, but widowhood was not to be recommended without the funds to support this status. Widows generally fell into three categories. There were those who went to live with a married son or daughter, like Philippa Olive who was over eighty in 1841 and living with her son William, his wife and their five children.

Then there were those who managed to keep their independence, usually by working, like Mary Kempe at the Bell, Ann Westcott, a lead smelter's widow, who became a nurse, and Jane Hocking, who was teaching at the Lead Works school in 1851. Another widow who remained in charge of her home was Elizabeth Pengelly. She presided over one of the larger households on the Green for many years. In 1841, when she was in her fifties, she had two daughters, a son-in-law Thomas Martyn, his brother, three grandchildren and a lodger, all living with her. Twenty years later she was still there with her daughter Susan Martyn and husband, Thomas, their eight children, as well as her sailor son, John. She must have had a dominant personality to control this diverse group.

A third category of widows were those who received some sort of parish help. Elizabeth Clymo, living in Point in 1851, is described on the census returns as a "pauper, formerly agricultural labourer's wife." Presumably she was being supported by the parish poor rates. But it was in Penpol where this help was most obvious.

Bridge Cottage, Penpol, once Lowarth Chyandour, a house for the poor

The Unknown Donor's Charity

The pretty, white-washed Bridge Cottage by Penpol Bridge, was once known as Lowarth Chyandoure. This could be translated as "Garden House by the Water," which is very appropriate as its garden near the stream is lovingly cared for today. This was given to the parish of Feock, probably in 1635, by an unnamed person "towards the Relife of the poore people." It was divided into two or three cottages, which provided a roof over the heads of families and especially widows. In 1841 there were three households, two entirely female and the third with two elderly widows and two young men, probably lodgers. The head of this household was Elizabeth Knowles, widow of the parish clerk, who obviously had little money to live on and pay the £4 rent. In 1845 the overseers of the poor were told to summon her two sons, Thomas and Richard, to the next magistrates' meeting to explain why they did not maintain their mother. However they ignored this and it was decided to take action against them. How this ended is not clear, but in 1851 she was living there with her son, Richard, a lead smelter, so perhaps this was the solution.

Between the two world wars, this property was sold, but the unknown donor's charity still exists and small amounts of money are distributed every year.

Widows left on their own with a family to bring up, might need to do work more usually done by the menfolk. This could include digging out the earth closet. Charles Hall's widow, after her husband's death from the effects of mustard gas poisoning in the 1st World War, would dig out the pit every spring behind their 3-holer lavatory, which was up a steep garden path. She then mixed this well-matured refuse with ashes to put in the potato trench, no doubt with handsome results.

SHOPS

The women did not need to go far to buy food, even if choice might be limited. Gardens provided some vegetables and fruit, which later the market gardens could also supply. Milk and butter came from the farms, and in the earlier years of this century a grocer's horse and waggon would come from Truro, taking orders one week and delivering the following week. Blewetts the baker and a milk cart also did the rounds. In addition there were the village shops.

One hundred and thirty years ago James Crago had his grocery shop just below the Green, and later another was opened on the top corner of the Green. Ned Bath and his wife took over this shop in about 1890 and ran it for nearly fifty years. "Aunt Bath's shop", as it was known, was a very friendly place, with its tinkling bell and its shelves stocked with the usual conglomeration of a village stores, flour, sugar, tea, cotton thread, matches and of course the sweets beloved by the children. It was a favourite place to catch up on all the gossip of the area.

Ferrris' coal yard and grocery shop opened on the quay between the wars, but now the coal store is a "desirable residence," and this shop and the later one on the Green, run by David Rees and his wife, have also closed so that none exists today.

A MUSICAL CONCLUSION

Much of this is looking at families from the outside, with little that is warm and personal. But music seems to be a theme that ran through the life of the area. In 1841, Point had Nicholas Dunstan, a blind musician, to provide music for celebrations; then the chapel choir was started, Bessie Chellew showed her skills as a pianist, concerts were held, and for a time in the 1920s, there was the Bleak House Band to give some oompah to events. But there is a more intimate picture of the importance of music, with the description of the family of Clarinda Trethowan, daughter of Edward and Caroline Bath of Trolver and Ned Bath's older sister. They lived for some years at Grove's End, just above the Penpol Valley at Four Turnings when John Trethowan, a master mariner, was often away at sea. This is their granddaughter's description of a family evening.

"Clarinda and her four daughters would sit in the lamplight, their voiders (work-baskets) beside them, planning their outfits for any important occasions in the coming spring and summer, and fitting each other and sewing. They had many callers, even in the winter, but when alone they were never at a loss to entertain themselves, belonging as they did to a generation to whom conversation was an art.....And very often in a lull in the chattering, one of the girls would softly start to sing, and the others would take up the tune. The rather unusual thing about their voices as a family was that most of the girls had deep contralto voices and the sons were nearly all tenors. This made for rather unique harmony when they all sang together, and when these rare times did occur they could go on for hours - and did. Every Sunday evening after church they would gather round the harmonium, and with their mother playing, sing all their favourite hymns, always ending with the one their father loved most."

Point and Penpol photographed by P. Strings in 1992. See also page 111.

105

Although William did not continue his direct involvement in the shipping line, he obviously followed the voyages with interest and whenever one of his son's ships came into Falmouth, a flag would flutter from his flagpole outside his house on the Green. (See Charles Rees' painting of Point Green.)

The Bell originally used on the Chellew ship, S.S. Penpol.
For some years, until it was stolen, this bell summoned the ferryman at Restronguet Passage.

Emotions ran high in Point in the mid-1890s when William caused some obstruction on the road by the Green, obviously making it difficult for people to get by. Letters were written, solicitors consulted and the newly-formed Parish Council discussed the problem. The matter had to be dealt wih delicately, and William Teague, manager of the tinworks, and Charles Rees suggested that it should go before the new District Council. This buck-passing was welcomed by the rest of the Parish Council, but it did not solve the problem. The obstruction still remained. The parish council then decided to pay men to remove it and send the bill of £1 10s to William. He did not pay it, so the council settled it and were annoyed enough to consider suing him. However, it was pointed out that the costs for this would be greater than the amount owing. Discussion still raged and how the question was finally resolved the minutes do not record. Such is village life.

In Feock church there are three memorial windows to the Chellews, one for William, one for his wife, Elizabeth, who died six years before him, and one for Richard, who died thirteen years after his father. In spite of this connection with the Anglican church, the family also had an active involvement with the Methodist chapel. William and his wife had both subscribed towards it at the time of the building of the chapel in 1861 and gave more on later occasions. When their daughters grew up they all became teachers in the Sunday School and undertook various responsibilities.

The eldest daughter, Honor, is first recorded as a teacher in 1872 when she was eighteen. She attended meetings regularly and collected money in Point for the tea treats. She was joined by her younger sister, Bessie, and they were given the job of arranging the music and singing for the Anniversary celebrations of 1876. Bessie later became one of the librarians with the task of choosing suitable new books. By the time Katie was a regular teacher, Honor had left, presumably to be married. Katie was married in Feock church in 1888. Perhaps her parents disapproved of their new son-in-law, Robert Hearle Martin, described as an "agricultural labourer," because they did not act as witnesses at the wedding. When Bessie married William Woolcock, a mining engineer, five years later in the Wesleyan chapel in Truro, both of her parents were present.

The *West Briton* report on William's death ended, "...he leaves two sons, Mr. Richard Chellew, Truro, and Mr. John Chellew J.P. of Cardiff." No mention was made of his daughters, yet Bessie, Mrs. Chellew Woolcock, was certainly still alive and active in Point. Perhaps the daughters were not considered important enough for a mention!

William was living in Point when Britain was at peace with most of her European neighbours, and building up the greatest maritime empire in the world. He contributed to the busy mercantile life of the county and experienced the spectacular rise and crash of Cornish copper mining. He saw railways come to Cornwall, the start of the motor car and perhaps wondered at one of the new-fangled flying machines. He was born eight years before Victoria became queen and outlived her by fifteen years. He died when Europe was being torn by the most terrible war yet fought, and when Britain's economic dominance was under threat. His life spanned some of the greatest changes ever known.

They were changes in which Point and Penpol had played a significant part.

INDEX OF FAMILY NAMES

110

*Another of P. Strings' aerial photographs taked in 1992.
(See also page 105.)*

WRITTEN SOURCES OF INFORMATION

Some sources have been indicated in the text; this list includes these as well as many of the others consulted.

Abbreviations used: C.R.O.   Cornwall Record Office
                     R.I.C.   Royal Institution of Cornwall
                     T.C.L   Truro City Reference Library
                     C.S.C.   Cornish Studies Centre, Redruth

General Sources

Feock Local History Booklets Nos. 1-4 (now out of print.)
Lake's Parochial History of the County of Cornwall
Life in Cornwall 1-4 R.M. Barton   D.B.Barton
Feock Parish Registers (C.R.O.)
Census Returns 1841-1891 (T.C.L).
Local Newspapers (T.C.L., R.I.C., C.S.C.)
Chapel Record Books Penpoll Methodist Church
Trade directories - Harrods and Kelly (T.C.L.)
St. Feock of the Past - manuscript Marion Chegwyn Penpoll Methodist Church
Clarinda - transcript - J.A.C.Ritchie, about her grandmother Clarinda Bath.
Gravestones - Feock Churchyard

Chapter One

Charles Henderson - Topography Vol. 3 - Feock (R.I.C.)
Cornish Place-Name Elements Oliver Padel English Place-Name Society 1985
Domestic Archaeology of Cornwall - Inst. of Cornish Studies 1979
Restronguet Creek - Old Cornwall 1979 Graves-Morris
Tithe Agreement, Feock DDP 64/3/1 (C.R.O.)
Tithe Apportionment 1841 and Tithe Map 1842 (C.R.O.)
Leases for Penpol Farm. DDWH 1479-89 (C.R.O.)
Leases for Chycoose. DDCY 1930-31,1993,(C.R.O.)
                    DDTLP 306-7 (C.R.O.)
Lease for Bone Mill   DDWH 1494-55 (C.R.O.)
Lease for Lynwood
Feock Parish Registers (C.R.O.)
Feock Church Book DDP 64/5/2 (C.R.O.)

Chapter Two

Cornish Shipwrecks: The North Coast Clive Carter Pan Books 1970
News From Cornwall A.K. Hamilton Jenkin Westaway Books 1951
Old Cornish Inns H.L. Douch D.Bradford Barton 1966
The Redruth and Chasewater Railway D.B.Barton 1966
Through Cornwall By Coach 1795 ed. D. Spreadbury 1971
Leases for Penpol Farm (C.R.O.) as above.
Letter from John Swan - transcript Carnon Downs Old Cornwall Society
J.S.T. Shipwreck Restronguet Creek Society Newsletter 1992 Barry Simpson
Lizzie R. Wilce R.I.C. Newsletter No. 11 George Hogg
Truro Roads 1700-1900 - transcript M.E. Philbrick (R.I.C.)

Chapter Three

The British Lead Mining Industry Roger Burt Dyllansow Truran 1984
Leases for the Lead Smelting Works WH 1496-7 (C.R.O.)

Chapter Four

Tin in Antiquity R.D. Penhallurick   The Institute of Metals 1986

The Metalliferous Mining Region of S.W. England H.G. Dines H.M.S.O. 1956
Mines and Miners of Cornwall A.K. Hamilton Jenkin Truro Bookshop 1967
Essays in Mining History Vol. 2 D.B. Barton 1970
Paper given by Charles Taylor to the Institute of Mechanics Penzance - Transcript - Carnon Downs Old Cornwall Society

Chapter Five

Essays in Mining History Vol. 2 D.B. Barton 1970
Devoran A Different Cornish Village B. Simpson
Leases for the Tin Smelting Works DDWH 1498-1503 (C.R.O)

Chapter Six

History of the Fal Working Boats Alun Davies 1989
Living History Under Sail ed. J. MacDonald
The Falmouth Working Boats Vol.2 Falmouth Working Boats Association
The Merchant Schooners Basil Greenhill Conway Maritime Press
Shipbuilding Data Researched by George Hogg
Shipowners P.N. Tregoning - transcript - Carnon Downs Old Cornwall Society
National Maritime Museum   Cotehele Quay

Chapter Seven

First three of previous section.
Close to the Earth Judith Cook Routledge and Kegan Paul 1984

Chapter Eight

The Cornish Miner in Australia Philip Payton Dyllansow Truran 1984
The Cornish in America A.L. Rowse Dyllansow Truran
Emigrant Lists (R.I.C.)

Chapter Ten

Smuggling in Devon and Cornwall Mary Waugh Countryside Books 1991
A Book About Smuggling A.D. Hippisley Coxe Tabb House 1984

Chapter Eleven

History Around the Fal   Part 3 Fal Local History Group
Treasurer's Account Book for Penpoll Chapel 1861-1912 Penpoll Methodist Church
Sunday School Teachers' Minute Books   "
Sunday School Teachers' Registers   "
Record of Pew Rents   "
Restronguet Creek Society Newsletter 1992

Chapter Twelve

Sunday School Teachers' Minute Books

Chapter Thirteen

Charles Rees' letter and Richard Harris' invoice Penpoll Methodist Church
Feock Parish Registers (C.R.O.)

Chapter Fourteen

Cymru A'r Mor No. 15 1992 (R.I.C.)
Chellew Line - transcript - R. Hall (R.I.C.)
Feock Vestry Records DDP 64/8/1 (C.R.O.)
Land Leases AD 201/9/1-2 (C.R.O.)
St. Ives Parish Registers (C.R.O.)